Quinoa
CUISINE

JUN 1 4 2012

Quinoa
CUISINE

150 Creative Recipes for Super-Nutritious,
Amazingly Delicious Dishes

Jessica Harlan & Kelley Sparwasser

Ulysses Press

Published by:
ULYSSES PRESS
P.O. Box 3440
Berkeley, CA 94703
www.ulyssespress.com

ISBN: 978-1-61243-020-1
Library of Congress Catalog Number 2011934776

Printed in Canada by Webcom

10 9 8 7 6 5 4 3 2 1

Acquisitions editor: Kelly Reed
Managing editor: Claire Chun
Editors: Lauren Harrison, Phyllis Elving
Proofreader: Elyce Berrigan-Dunlop
Production: Judith Metzener
Cover design: what!design @ whatweb.com
Front cover photographs: Bowls of quinoa © FOOD-images/fotolia.com; pancakes
    © Elena Elisseeva/shutterstock.com; falafel © bonchan/shutterstock.com
Back cover photographs: Blini © Robyn Mackenzie/shutterstock.com; carrot cake
    © RoJo Images/shutterstock.com
Interior images all from shutterstock.com: Crayon © Miguel Angel Salinas Salinas;
    glasses © Samer; heart © zphoto; leaf © SiuWing; milk and eggs © Feliks
    Kogan; radish © Casablanca; refrigerator © stoyanh; snowflake © SiuWing;
    sprout © SiuWing; sun © SiuWing ; timer © Samer; wheat © LHF Graphics

Distributed by Publishers Group West

For Chip, Sadie, and Gillian, my all-time favorite dining companions.
—*JH*

In loving memory of my grandmother Agnes, who taught me how to cook.
—*KS*

Contents

Introduction

In a time when the term "superfood" is bandied about with alacrity, it's worth noting that quinoa is truly deserving of that designation. It's been said that quinoa is one of the few foods that can provide nearly all the nutrients essential for life. Because quinoa is so nutritious, NASA has even done research on its viability as a crop to cultivate in space.

Although quinoa (pronounced *KEEN-wah*) is enjoying a surge in popularity because it's so healthful and versatile, it's certainly nothing new. In fact, quinoa has a lengthy and dramatic history.

The ancient Incans revered quinoa, referring to it as "gold" or the "mother crop." With great ceremony, the Incan leader planted the first seeds each year using a golden shovel, and celebrations surrounded the harvest. In the Andean mountain region of what is now parts of Peru, Bolivia, Ecuador, Argentina, and Chile, quinoa was important both for sustenance and as part of the culture—until Spanish explorer Francisco Pizarro destroyed the fields and declared quinoa illegal in the effort to conquer the Incans. Quinoa very nearly vanished along with the Incan civilization.

Luckily, wild quinoa survived in the mountains of Peru and Bolivia, and some was cultivated for personal use by small-scale farmers far away from the Spanish-occupied area. By 1825, after the Spanish American countries had won their independence and quinoa was no longer illegal, it was still considered the food of the poor and provincial. Even today many South Americans—particularly young Bolivians—look down on quinoa, preferring "new" cultivated grains introduced by the Europeans, such as wheat.

The California-based Quinoa Corporation (which today sells quinoa under the brand Ancient Harvest) introduced quinoa commercially to Americans in the late 1980s, and the National Association of Quinoa Producers was formed in Bolivia in 1983 to help organize the quinoa supply chain. Today there are about fifty importers of quinoa in the United States, along with a handful of domestic producers. In recent years quinoa has been "rediscovered" as a valuable grain for its high nutritional value and its hardiness (quinoa has been known to survive—and even thrive—during major droughts that have wiped out other crops). American and European foreign-aid organizations have been helping farmers in South America cultivate quinoa for exportation.

What Is Quinoa?

Although quinoa often gets classified as a grain, like wheat and barley, it's actually in the goosefoot family, related to beets, spinach, and chard. The seed of the plant is what's most commonly consumed. (The leaves also can be eaten, but they're not commonly found in

U.S. stores.) Nutritionists refer to quinoa as a "pseudograin" (along with amaranth and buck-wheat) because it has a similar nutritional profile to true grains and is prepared and served in similar ways.

Most of the world's supply of quinoa is still grown in the Andes region of South America, although the plant is starting to be cultivated in the United States and Canada, in mountainous areas that have similar cold and dry conditions.

Quinoa plants are bushy stalks that can grow as tall as nine feet, with large seed heads. There are hundreds of known varieties, but the most commonly available are white, red, and black. The quinoa seeds are covered in saponin, a bitter coating that agriculturists believe helps protect the seeds from insects and birds—making quinoa a particularly easy crop to grow without the use of chemical pesticides. Quinoa processors typically use either a water bath or mechanical abrasion to remove the saponin.

Quinoa's Health Benefits

Quinoa has a nutritional profile that few other plant products can match. You can reap some of these nutritional benefits by substituting the seeds for less nourishing foods. Use quinoa instead of white rice or couscous in pilafs, for example, or incorporate quinoa flour or flakes into baked goods in place of all or part of the wheat flour.

According to NutritionData.com, one serving of quinoa (185 grams or 6½ ounces) has the following nutritional content, as compared to the same volume of white rice and pearled barley:

	COOKED QUINOA (1 CUP/185G)	COOKED WHITE RICE (1 CUP/174G)	COOKED PEARLED BARLEY (1 CUP/182G)
Calories	222	169	193
Fat	4g	0g	1g
Protein	8g	4g	4g
Sodium	12mg	9mg	5mg
Carbohydrates	39g	37g	44g
Dietary Fiber	5g	2g	6g
Sugar	8g	0g	0g
Calcium	31.5mg	3.5mg	17.3mg
Iron	12.8mg	0.2mg	2.1mg
Folate	77.7mcg	1.7mcg	25.2mcg
Magnesium	118mg	8.7mg	34.5mg
Phosphorous	281mg	13.9mg	84.8mg
Potassium	318mg	17.4mg	146mg

Here are some of the nutritional benefits you'll enjoy by making the quinoa recipes in this book:

- Quinoa is rich in protein, calcium, iron, fiber, and potassium (which helps control blood pressure), and it is a good source of B vitamins and vitamin E. It's considered a complete protein because it provides a healthy balance of all eight essential amino acids, one of the few plant foods that does so.

- The germ in quinoa seeds makes up about 60 percent of the grain, yielding a high ratio of protein to carbohydrates. Quinoa is higher in protein than rice, corn, or wheat, and higher in fiber than corn or wheat. This nutritional profile means that quinoa can help you feel full longer than many other foods, making it ideal for trying to maintain a healthy weight.

- People with celiac disease and others who are sensitive to gluten, wheat, and other grass-based food products will find quinoa useful because it is gluten-free. Quinoa contains more antioxidants than gluten-free products made with rice, corn, or potato, so incorporating quinoa flour into gluten-free baked goods gives them a big nutritional boost.

- Research has also shown that quinoa may be useful in preventing certain diseases. Because it's rich in the antioxidant quercetin, it may be helpful in managing type-2 diabetes and associated hypertension. In one study, quinoa was shown to reverse certain adverse effects of a high-fructose diet on lipids and glucose levels in lab animals.

Types of Quinoa and Quinoa Products

There are a number of quinoa types and products on the market. Here are the most common:

White Quinoa   Also called ivory or yellow quinoa, this is the most readily available type of quinoa, sold in most supermarkets in the natural foods section. Some people describe the flavor as "nutty." White quinoa has the mildest flavor of all the varieties and is neutral enough to take on the flavors of other ingredients. The texture of cooked white quinoa can be al dente (with a slight firmness, like pasta) or slightly mushy, depending on how long it's cooked and in how much liquid. This is typically the least expensive type of quinoa.

Red Quinoa   A beautiful mahogany red, this quinoa has a nuttier flavor than the white type, and a slightly chewier texture. It makes a great accent, in terms of both color and texture, in stews or other longer-cooked recipes, as it holds its shape and firmness better than

SPROUTING QUINOA

Sprouting quinoa is easy, and it's believed to boost some of the seed's health benefits. Quinoa sprouts can be added to salads, sandwiches, and an array of other cold dishes.

Rinse the quinoa, rubbing it between your fingers to remove any remaining saponin. Place in a shallow dish and add enough water to cover the quinoa by at least 1 inch. Cover the dish with a clean dish towel and let stand at room temperature for 45 minutes to 1 hour. Then place the quinoa in a strainer, gently rinse, and drain off the excess water. Return the quinoa to the shallow dish and spread in an even layer. Cover with a clean dish towel and place in a cool, dark place for 8 to 12 hours.

At this point the quinoa will have begun to sprout and may be eaten. However, if you'd like longer sprouts, you can continue to let them grow. Place them in a strainer, gently rinse, and drain off excess water. Return the sprouting quinoa to the shallow dish, spread in an even layer, again cover with a clean dish towel, and place in a cool, dark place for another 8 to 12 hours. You can repeat this process another time or two, if you wish.

Once the sprouts are the length you want, rinse them and then store in the refrigerator, covered, for 1 to 3 days. (The longer you left the quinoa to sprout, the sooner you should use them.)

In our tests, we found that quinoa sprouts will quickly mold and spoil if the water isn't drained thoroughly after rinsing and if the quinoa is left for more than 12 hours between rinses.

white quinoa. Red quinoa is a little more difficult to find than white and can be pricier. Look for it online or in specialty or natural food stores.

Black Quinoa   Actually more dark brown than black, this quinoa has the firmest texture of the three varieties. It has a seedlike crunchiness when cooked and a more pronounced flavor than either red or white quinoa. Some people describe it as earthy; we think it's reminiscent of black tea and complements Asian dishes particularly well.

Tri-color Quinoa   A combination of white, red, and black quinoa that's sometimes labeled as rainbow quinoa, this mixture is available packaged or in bulk. The blend is sometimes less expensive than pure red or black quinoa. Use it to give a lovely, colorful appearance to a recipe.

Quinoa Flakes   Often found next to oatmeal and other hot cereals in the supermarket or natural food store, quinoa flakes are produced by steaming white quinoa and rolling it into tiny disks. The flakes look a bit like rolled oats and cook faster than regular quinoa. They're best used in porridge, as a substitute for bread crumbs in coatings or toppings, or incorporated into baked goods. The flakes have a mild, neutral flavor.

Quinoa Flour   Available in the baking or natural foods section of the supermarket or at a natural food store, quinoa flour is an excellent way to make baked goods a little more nutritious. The flour can vary in color from off-white to light brown, so it may make batter or dough a little darker than if made with wheat flour. It also produces a denser, heavier texture. Because quinoa flour is gluten-free, it won't rise in bread dough the same way wheat flour does. Unless you're baking gluten-free, try using it in place of up to half of the wheat flour until you're familiar with the results.

Quinoa flour has a slightly grassy flavor that some might consider bitter. In our recipes, we've tried to work to complement, rather than mask, the unique flavor.

Shopping for Quinoa

Because most quinoa is imported, and because it's gaining in popularity, it can be a pricey ingredient. But quinoa does triple in volume when cooked, so you get more from less, compared to most grains. Here are some tips for cutting the cost of quinoa:

- **Buy in bulk.** Seek out a natural food store that has bulk bins for dry goods. Typically quinoa is less expensive when bought in bulk rather than prepackaged.

- **Shop at a wholesale club.** Some of the lowest-priced quinoa we found was at our local Costco stores. The 4-pound bags sold there provide enough to last for months, even for a large family or avid quinoa eaters!

- **Buy online.** Many quinoa manufacturers sell their products online, so you can have it delivered directly to your door. See Quinoa Manufacturers and Resources (page 209) for some of our favorite quinoa websites.

- **Buy white quinoa.** White quinoa is the most common and least expensive of the varietals. Use it in place of red or black quinoa in recipes if you're trying to economize.

- **Make your own flour.** Quinoa flour often costs twice as much as regular quinoa. If you have a grain mill, you can easily grind dry quinoa to make your own flour.

Quinoa Cooking Methods and Tips

One of the most appealing attributes of quinoa is that it cooks so quickly—in about 15 minutes. We've found that there are a number of ways to cook quinoa successfully. Experiment with different methods until you find the one that gives you the results you prefer in terms of firmness and texture.

These are the techniques that have worked the best for us:

Rinsing Quinoa Most companies prewash their quinoa to remove the outer coating of saponin, but we suggest an additional rinse to remove any potentially bitter remnants. Place the measured amount of uncooked quinoa in a fine-mesh sieve or colander. Rinse under cool running water, rubbing the quinoa between your fingers as you do so. Shake the sieve over the sink a few times to drain excess water before cooking the quinoa.

Quinoa to Liquid Ratio In general, we suggest 1 part quinoa to 2 parts liquid, whether you are using white, red, or black quinoa. This means:

UNCOOKED QUINOA	LIQUID (WATER OR STOCK)	COOKED QUINOA YIELD
¼ cup	½ cup	¾ cup
⅓ cup	⅔ cup	1 cup
½ cup	1 cup	1½ cups
⅔ cup	1⅓ cups	2 cups
¾ cup	1½ cups	2¼ cups
1 cup	2 cups	3 cups

For firmer, drier quinoa, use less liquid (such as 1 cup quinoa to 1¾ cup water) and a shorter cooking time.

Stovetop Method 1

We predominately use the following method throughout this book:

In a small or medium saucepan over high heat, bring the quinoa and water, stock, or broth to a boil. Reduce the heat to low, cover, and cook until the water has been absorbed and the quinoa is tender, 10 to 12 minutes for white quinoa, 18 to 20 minutes for red or black. Turn off the heat and let the quinoa sit, covered, for 5 minutes. Fluff with a fork.

Be sure to bring the liquid to a full boil or the quinoa may be undercooked and the water may not be completely absorbed. Should this happen, simply set the saucepan over medium heat and cook 5 minutes longer.

Stovetop Method 2 ("Pasta" Method)

Should you be particularly sensitive to the bitterness of saponin, the "pasta" method provides an additional "rinse," since the cooking water is drained off after cooking. This method yields the same amount of cooked quinoa as the basic stovetop method, but it uses a ratio of 1 part quinoa to 4 parts liquid.

In a medium or large saucepan over medium-high to high heat, bring the water, stock, or broth to a boil. Add the quinoa and cook, uncovered, until tender, 12 to 14 minutes. Drain in a fine-mesh sieve or colander. Transfer to a bowl and fluff with a fork.

Rice Cooker Method

Place 1 part quinoa and 2 parts water, stock, or broth in the bowl of a rice cooker and follow the manufacturer's instructions for cooking white rice. Quinoa triples in volume when cooked, so be sure to leave room in the rice cooker to accommodate the increased volume. Fluff the quinoa with a fork once it's completely cooked.

Oven Method

Preheat the oven to 350°F. Bring 2 parts water, stock, or broth to a boil in a saucepan on the stovetop. Place 1 part uncooked quinoa in an ovenproof dish large enough to accommodate the increase in volume. Pour the boiling liquid over the quinoa and cover with a lid or aluminum foil. Bake until the liquid has been absorbed and the quinoa is tender, 30 to 35 minutes.

Microwave Method

In a microwave-safe bowl large enough to accommodate the volume of the cooked quinoa, place 1 part quinoa and 2 parts water, stock, or broth. Cover with plastic wrap or a lid; cook on high power for 10 minutes. Stir the quinoa and scrape down the sides with a spatula so that no quinoa sticks to the side of the bowl above the water line. Continue to cook, covered, at 60 percent power (power level 6) for 12 more minutes. Let stand for 5 minutes, then fluff with a fork.

A NOTE ABOUT NUTRITIONAL INFORMATION

We've provided nutritional information in this book for educational purposes. While we've done our best to provide accurate information, we are not professional nutritionists or dieticians. If you have any questions about including quinoa in your diet, you should consult your health care provider or another licensed professional.

About the Recipes

Within each chapter of this book, the recipes are organized by the seasons of the year. To make use of seasonal ingredients, look for the season icons on each page: winter is a snowflake, spring is a seedling, summer is a sun, and fall is a leaf.

Recipes also are identified with icons to help you decide which dish is appropriate for which occasion. Look for the following icons throughout the book:

 30 Minutes or Less   Quick and easy to make, from prepping the ingredients to bringing the finished dish to the table.

 Freezes Well   Can be made ahead, placed in a freezer-safe container, and stored in the freezer until ready to serve.

 Gluten-Free   Contains no wheat products. Please note that although we've done our best to make sure these recipes contain no gluten, you should double-check ingredient labels or consult your health care provider if you need to avoid gluten for medical reasons.

 Good for Company   Wonderful for a special-occasion meal. These recipes might use special techniques, include fancy ingredients, or simply be good large-scale dishes to serve at a dinner party.

 Healthy Choice   Low in fat or full of nutritional ingredients such as fiber, whole grains, fruits, or vegetables.

 Kid Friendly   Mild and kid-pleasing in flavor and texture, and often easy enough that kids can help prepare the recipes.

 Vegan   Contains no dairy, meat, eggs, honey, or other animal product. (Double-check the labels of any packaged ingredients to make sure they don't include animal products.)

 Vegetarian   Contains no animal meat but may contain dairy products or eggs. (Double-check the labels of any packaged ingredients to make sure they don't contain meat.)

CHAPTER 1
Essential Recipes

These twelve basic recipes are great on their own, but as you cook your way through this book, you'll see how they find their way into other dishes. We encourage you to use these basics to inspire your own creations.

Quinoa Porridge

Quinoa Buttermilk Pancakes

Quinoa Crepes

Quinoa Buttermilk Biscuits

Quinoa Tortillas

Quinoa Muffins

Quinoa Frying Batter

Quinoa Stuffing

Quinoa Pilaf

Quinoa Pizza Dough

Quinoa–Rice Flour Pie Crust

Quinoa–Whole Wheat Pie Crust

QUINOA PORRIDGE

There are few better ways to begin the morning than with a bowl of hearty, filling, nourishing porridge. Try different kinds of sweeteners and spices, stir in dried fruits, or top with a sprinkling of nuts to get your day off to a great start.   **SERVES 4**

1 cup white, red, or black quinoa, rinsed

1 cup water

1 cup whole, reduced-fat, or skim milk

1 tablespoon sweetener, such as brown sugar, maple syrup, or honey

½ teaspoon ground cinnamon or other ground baking spices

1. In a medium saucepan, combine the quinoa, water, and milk. Bring to a simmer over medium heat. Stir in the sweetener and cinnamon or other ground spices. Reduce the heat to low, cover, and simmer for 15 minutes. Turn off the heat and let sit, covered, for 5 minutes.

2. Give the quinoa a few stirs, then spoon into individual bowls and serve hot.

TO BEAT EGG WHITES

Beating egg whites can be tricky. Follow these tips to ensure lofty peaks:

- Make certain your bowl and beaters are clean and dry.

- Have your eggs at room temperature.

- Make sure no yolk gets into the whites when you separate them, as it will prevent the egg whites from reaching their full volume. Should part of the yolk get into the whites, use the empty shell to scoop it out.

- Cream of tartar—⅛ teaspoon per egg white—helps the beaten egg whites hold their form. Add the cream of tartar once the egg whites begin to foam.

QUINOA BUTTERMILK PANCAKES

A great go-to pancake recipe plus a few simple additions—your favorite fruit, or shredded coconut and macadamia nuts for a Hawaiian twist—will jazz up any breakfast. You can also give this recipe a savory slant by adding chopped fresh herbs, cheese, or seasonings such as cumin or paprika. Unlike traditional pancake recipes, here you beat the egg whites before adding them to the batter, which helps keep the quinoa flour from making the pancakes dense. MAKES 8 TO 10 PANCAKES

¾ cup quinoa flour

¾ cup quinoa flakes

½ teaspoon kosher salt

1 teaspoon baking powder

1½ teaspoons baking soda

2 large eggs, at room temperature

3 tablespoons honey

¾ cup buttermilk

¼ teaspoon cream of tartar

unsalted butter, as needed

1. In a bowl, stir together the quinoa flour, quinoa flakes, salt, baking powder, and baking soda.

2. Separate the egg whites and yolks into two medium bowls; set aside the whites. Whisk the yolks together with the honey and buttermilk. Stir the flour mixture into the egg yolk mixture until combined. Set aside for 5 minutes.

3. Beat the egg whites with an electric mixer on low speed until they begin to foam, about 1 minute. Add the cream of tartar, increase the speed to medium-high and continue beating until firm peaks form, 1 to 2 minutes longer. Using a rubber spatula, gently fold the egg whites into the batter until just combined.

4. Heat a griddle or a large nonstick skillet over medium heat. Add a dollop of butter and melt, spreading with a large flat spatula or tilting to coat the skillet completely. Spoon the batter onto the griddle or skillet, about ⅓ cup per pancake. Cook until the underside is golden and the edges appear dry, 5 to 7 minutes, then flip and cook through, about 5 minutes longer. Repeat with the rest of the batter, adding more butter as needed. You can keep cooked pancakes warm in a 170°F oven while you cook the rest.

QUINOA CREPES

Quinoa flour creates a sturdy crepe, ideal for stuffing. For a more delicate version, reduce the quinoa flour to ½ cup. If you're making a sweet crepe, add 1½ teaspoons of granulated sugar to this batter; for a savory flavor, add chopped parsley and other fresh herbs. **MAKES 6 TO 8 CREPES**

2 large eggs

1 cup whole milk

1½ teaspoons grated lemon zest

1 cup quinoa flour

pinch kosher salt

unsalted butter, as needed

1. In a medium bowl, beat the eggs until combined, then whisk in the milk and lemon zest. Stir in the quinoa flour and salt.

2. Heat a 10-inch crepe pan or nonstick skillet over medium-high heat. Add a dollop of butter and melt, tilting to coat the pan or spreading with a large, flat spatula. Pour in ¼ cup of batter and either tilt the pan in a circular motion or spread the batter with a wooden ratêau (crepe spreader) to coat the pan. Cook until the underside has browned, about 2 minutes. Flip and cook 1 to 2 minutes longer. Repeat with the remaining batter. Keep the cooked crepes warm in a 170°F oven until ready to serve.

QUINOA BUTTERMILK BISCUITS

Since Jessica lives in Atlanta, we simply couldn't resist including a buttermilk biscuit recipe—a staple in Southern cuisine. Our version, a quick drop biscuit, uses a technique we learned from the folks at the popular Pine State Biscuits restaurant in Portland, Oregon: freezing and grating the butter, resulting in an especially tender biscuit. Place the butter in the freezer 15 to 20 minutes before you prepare the dough. These biscuits are best served warm with butter and jam or honey. **MAKES 12 BISCUITS**

1 cup quinoa flakes

1 cup all-purpose flour

2 tablespoons granulated sugar

½ teaspoon kosher salt

1 tablespoon baking powder

1 teaspoon baking soda

4 tablespoons frozen unsalted butter

1½ cups buttermilk

1. In a medium bowl, stir together the quinoa flakes, flour, sugar, salt, baking powder, and baking soda.

2. Remove the butter from the freezer and grate, using the large holes of the grater. Add half the grated butter to the flour mixture and toss with a fork to coat with the dry ingredients, making sure the butter doesn't clump. Repeat with the remaining butter.

3. Add half the buttermilk, quickly stir to combine, and repeat with the remaining buttermilk. Be careful not to overwork the dough. The dough will be wet. Cover and refrigerate for 30 minutes.

4. Preheat the oven to 350°F. Line a rimmed baking sheet with parchment paper.

5. Use a ¼ cup measuring cup to scoop the dough onto the prepared baking sheet, leaving 1½ to 2 inches between biscuits. Bake about 15 minutes, until the biscuits are golden brown on top and a cake tester inserted into a biscuit comes out with only a few crumbs clinging to it. Leave on the pan to cool on a wire rack for 10 minutes, then transfer the biscuits directly to the wire rack to cool completely. Store in an airtight container at room temperature for 1 to 2 days.

QUINOA TORTILLAS

The quinoa flour and butter in these tortillas adds a slight nutty flavor and richness not found in traditional corn tortillas. It's best to use a tortilla press to form the dough, but if you don't have one, roll out each disk of dough on a well-floured work surface using a floured rolling pin. MAKES 8 TO 16 TORTILLAS

1½ cups hot water, divided

1 cup quinoa flakes

1 cup masa harina

½ cup all-purpose flour

¾ teaspoon kosher salt

5 tablespoons unsalted butter, chilled and diced

1. In a medium bowl, stir together 1 cup of the hot water and the quinoa flakes. Let the flakes soak for 2 minutes.

2. Combine the masa harina, all-purpose flour, and salt in the bowl of a food processor and pulse to combine, about 10 pulses. Add the soaked quinoa flakes and process to combine, about 45 seconds. Add the butter and pulse until the mixture resembles coarse crumbs, with butter pieces about the size of small peas. Add the remaining ½ cup hot water and process until the dough begins to form a ball.

3. Turn the dough out onto a well-floured work surface and gently add any dough bits that haven't been incorporated into the ball. The dough should be slightly sticky; if necessary, add flour or water to create the right consistency. Press the dough into a disk, wrap in plastic, and refrigerate for 30 minutes or longer before forming the tortillas.

4. To make the tortillas, heat a cast-iron skillet over high heat. Cut the disk of dough into 8 to 16 equal-size pieces, according to the size of tortillas you want. Roll into small balls and flatten each one into a disk. Place a sheet of waxed paper on the bottom of a tortilla press; add a disk of dough and cover with another sheet of waxed paper. Lower the top of the press and apply firm pressure to flatten the dough; lift and remove the top

piece of waxed paper. Gently lift the tortilla from the press, using the bottom piece of waxed paper, and turn into the cast-iron skillet. Immediately remove the waxed paper so it doesn't melt onto the tortilla or the skillet. Cook until the underside begins to brown and blister, 1 to 2 minutes, then flip and cook on the second side until the tortilla begins to puff and the underside begins to brown and blister, 1 to 2 minutes longer. Remove. Repeat for the remaining pieces of dough. Keep warm in a 170°F oven until ready to serve.

Tortilla Chips Variation: Fill a large heavy pot, such as a Dutch oven, with canola oil to a depth of 4 to 6 inches. Heat to 350°F. Line a rimmed baking sheet with paper towels. Make the tortilla dough as instructed, cutting the disk of dough into 16 equal pieces. Flatten each piece on the tortilla press as instructed, then cut each tortilla into quarters and gently place in the oil, being careful not to splash the hot oil. Fry the dough until it has puffed and browned on the bottom, 45 seconds to 1 minute. Using tongs, flip the dough, then fry until the second side has browned, about 45 seconds longer. Remove the chips with a slotted spoon and drain on the prepared baking sheet. Sprinkle with salt. Serve hot or warm.

QUINOA MUFFINS

These muffins make for a great on-the-go breakfast or snack. While they're extremely tasty on their own, you can add blueberries, raspberries and lemon zest, dried cranberries and chopped walnuts, or almost anything you choose to create your own muffin masterpieces. **MAKES 12 MUFFINS**

1¼ cups quinoa flakes

1¼ cups all-purpose flour

¾ cup granulated sugar

½ teaspoon kosher salt

1 teaspoon baking powder

½ teaspoon baking soda

½ teaspoon ground cinnamon

¼ teaspoon grated nutmeg

4 tablespoons frozen unsalted butter

1 large egg

1 cup unsweetened applesauce

½ teaspoon vanilla extract

½ cup whole milk

1. Preheat the oven to 350°F. Spray 12 cups of a standard muffin pan with cooking spray.

2. In a medium bowl, stir together the quinoa flakes, flour, sugar, salt, baking powder, baking soda, cinnamon, and nutmeg.

3. Remove the butter from the freezer and grate, using the large holes of the grater. Add half the grated butter to the flour mixture and toss with a fork to coat with the dry ingredients, making sure the butter does not clump. Repeat with the remaining butter.

4. In a small bowl, whisk together the egg, applesauce, vanilla, and milk. Stir the flour mixture into the egg mixture until combined.

5. Spoon the batter evenly among the prepared muffin cups. Bake until the tops of the muffins are light brown and spring back when pressed lightly, 15 to 20 minutes. Cool in the pan on a wire rack for 10 minutes, then transfer the muffins directly to the wire rack to cool completely. Store at room temperature in a covered container for 1 to 2 days.

QUINOA FRYING BATTER

This light and simple batter is the perfect coating for frying an array of foods. Use it in place of tempura batter, or as a coating for salt and pepper calamari or coconut prawns. MAKES ½ CUP BATTER

canola oil, as needed for frying

¼ cup quinoa flour

¼ cup club soda

1 large egg, at room temperature

salt

1. Fill a large heavy pot, such as a Dutch oven, with oil to a depth about 3 inches greater than what you'll be frying. Heat to 350°F. Line a rimmed baking sheet with paper towels. In a medium bowl, whisk together the quinoa flour and club soda.

2. Separate the egg white from the yolk, placing the white in a second medium bowl and reserving the yolk for another use. Beat the egg white with an electric mixer on low speed until it begins to foam, about 1 minute. Increase the mixer speed to medium-high and beat until firm peaks form, 1 to 2 minutes longer. Using a spatula, gently fold the egg white into the quinoa flour mixture until just combined. Season with salt and use immediately.

3. Dip the item you are frying in the batter to coat and gently lower into the oil, being careful not to splash the hot oil. Cook, turning as needed, until all sides are golden brown. Using a slotted spoon, remove from the oil and drain on the prepared baking sheet. Season to taste with salt. Repeat for the remaining pieces to be fried.

QUINOA STUFFING

Whether you call it dressing or stuffing, this savory mix is a must-have alongside a Thanksgiving turkey or a weeknight roasted chicken. It's a healthier version of bread stuffing, with a less-gummy consistency. Better yet, the cooking temperature and time are forgiving—you can cook it right alongside the bird, no matter what temperature the oven is set at. Just be sure to adjust the cooking time and watch the stuffing carefully for doneness. You can cook this right in the ovenproof saucepan in which you simmer the quinoa, or transfer the whole mixture to a casserole dish for a nicer presentation on the dinner table. SERVES 4 TO 6 (ABOUT 3½ CUPS)

1 cup white quinoa, rinsed

¾ cup water

1 cup chicken or vegetable stock or broth

1 bay leaf

3 tablespoons unsalted butter, divided

2 ribs celery, minced

1 small onion, minced

2 tablespoons minced fresh sage

2 teaspoons dried thyme or 1 tablespoon fresh thyme, minced

kosher salt and black pepper

1. Preheat the oven to 350°F. In a medium ovenproof saucepan with a lid, combine the quinoa, water, stock or broth, and bay leaf. Bring to a simmer over medium heat, then reduce the heat to low, cover, and simmer until the quinoa is tender and the water has been absorbed, 10 to 12 minutes.

2. Meanwhile, in a medium skillet, melt 2 tablespoons of the butter. Add the celery and onion and sauté, stirring occasionally, until the vegetables are tender, 7 to 8 minutes. Stir in the sage and thyme.

3. When the quinoa is cooked, stir in the vegetables. Season to taste with salt and pepper. Smooth the mixture into an even layer and bake in the pan, covered, until just lightly browned around the edges, about 20 minutes. If you don't have an ovenproof saucepan, transfer the mixture to an 11 x 7-inch casserole dish with a lid (or cover with aluminum foil) to bake.

STUFFING SAFETY

If you plan to stuff a turkey or chicken with this quinoa stuffing, follow these tips for food safety:

- Prepare the stuffing just before filling the turkey, and stuff the bird while the stuffing is still warm. Cook the turkey immediately at an oven temperature no lower than 325°F.

- Stuff the bird loosely, using about ¾ cup stuffing per pound of turkey.

- The turkey and the stuffing should both reach an internal temperature of 165°F when checked with a meat thermometer. The cooked turkey should rest for 20 minutes before the stuffing is removed and the turkey is carved.

- Store leftovers in the refrigerator within 2 hours of cooking, and eat within 3 days. Be sure to reheat the leftovers (both the turkey and the stuffing) to at least 165°F before serving.

QUINOA PILAF

A less-predictable alternative to rice, quinoa pilaf is a versatile side dish that can be adapted according to whatever you're serving and whatever ingredients you have on hand. Experiment with different types of oil, aromatics (fragrant, flavorful veggies such as onions and shallots), liquids, herbs, and other ingredients. You'll never need to have the same dish twice. SERVES 4

1 tablespoon extra-virgin olive oil, canola oil, or vegetable oil

½ cup diced onion, shallots, or leeks

¾ cup white, red, or black quinoa, rinsed

1½ cup chicken or vegetable stock or broth

2 tablespoons chopped fresh herbs, such as parsley or tarragon (optional)

kosher salt and black pepper

1. In a medium saucepan, heat the oil over medium heat. Add the onion, shallots, or leeks and sauté, stirring frequently, until translucent, 5 to 7 minutes.

2. Add the quinoa and cook, stirring frequently, until the quinoa is fragrant and lightly toasted, 3 to 5 minutes.

3. Add the stock or broth and bring to a simmer. Cover, reduce heat to low, and simmer until the quinoa is tender and the liquid has been absorbed, 10 to 12 minutes. Turn off the heat and let the quinoa sit for 5 minutes. Fluff with a fork and season to taste with salt, pepper, and herbs, if using.

QUINOA PIZZA DOUGH

Adding quinoa flour to a classic pizza dough recipe adds not only some healthy protein but also a nice nuttiness to the crust. Use this dough for pizza (pages 129, 198) or calzones (page 151)—or, for an easy appetizer, simply flatten it, brush with olive oil, sprinkle with dried pizza seasoning, Parmesan cheese, and garlic powder, and bake at 400°F until golden, 12 to 15 minutes. You can also brush the flattened dough with olive oil and cook it right on a hot grill to make flatbread; cook it 2 to 3 minutes per side. MAKES DOUGH FOR ONE 1 2-INCH PIZZA

1¼ cups very warm water (about 110°F to 120°F)

1 tablespoon active dry yeast

1 tablespoon honey

2 to 2½ cups bread flour, as needed, divided

1 teaspoon kosher salt

1 tablespoon plus 1 teaspoon extra-virgin olive oil, divided

1½ cups quinoa flour

1. Place the warm water in a large bowl. Stir in the yeast, honey, and 1 cup bread flour. Let sit in a warm place until foamy, about 15 minutes.

2. Stir in the salt, 1 tablespoon olive oil, and quinoa flour. Gradually add the remaining bread flour, ½ cup at a time, until the dough forms a slightly sticky ball. Turn out onto a well-floured work surface and knead until smooth and elastic, about 10 minutes. Add more flour if needed. The dough will be slightly sticky. Form into a ball.

3. Drizzle the remaining 1 teaspoon olive oil into a clean bowl. Place the ball of dough in the bowl, turning to coat with oil. Cover the bowl with plastic wrap and let the dough rise in a warm place until nearly doubled in size, about 1 hour. Use in your favorite pizza or calzone recipe.

QUINOA–RICE FLOUR PIE CRUST

This crust—crumbly and almost like shortbread—is ideal for quiches, creamy pies, and potpies. For sweet fillings, add a tablespoon of granulated sugar with the flour. Be sure to spray or grease your pie dish to keep the crust from sticking. This pie crust can also be used in recipes that call for an uncooked crust, to be baked after being filled. **Makes One 9-inch Pie Crust**

¾ cup quinoa flour

⅓ cup rice flour

¼ cup arrowroot starch

¼ teaspoon kosher salt

½ cup (1 stick) cold unsalted butter, diced

¼ cup ice water

1. In a bowl, stir together the quinoa flour, rice flour, arrowroot starch, and salt. Add the butter and toss to coat. Use a pastry cutter, two knives, or your clean hands to work the butter into the flour until the mixture resembles coarse crumbs, with butter pieces about the size of peas.

2. Gradually add the ice water a tablespoon at a time, stirring with a fork until the dough comes together. Turn out onto a well-floured work surface and knead two or three times, just enough for the dough to form a ball. It should be slightly sticky; add more quinoa flour, rice flour, or ice water as needed to create the right consistency.

3. Press the dough into a disk, cover with plastic wrap, and refrigerate for at least 30 minutes before using.

4. To make a pie crust, preheat the oven to 400°F. Spray a 9-inch pie pan with cooking spray or grease with butter. Roll the chilled dough into a roughly 10- or 11-inch circle on a generously floured work surface, making sure the dough doesn't stick. Transfer to the prepared pan, trim any excess dough, and, if you wish, crimp the edges of the crust with your fingers or a fork for decoration. Prick the crust all over the bottom and sides with a fork, line the crust with aluminum foil, and fill the bottom of the crust with pie weights or dried beans to keep it from shrinking. Bake for about 10 minutes, remove the foil and weights, return to the oven, and continue to bake until golden, about 5 minutes longer. Fill as desired.

QUINOA–WHOLE WHEAT PIE CRUST

This crust is a bit easier to work with than the Quinoa–Rice Flour Pie Crust (page 30), since it includes wheat flour. Add 1 tablespoon granulated sugar if you're using the crust with a sweet filling. This pie crust can also be used in recipes that call for an uncooked crust to be filled and then baked. MAKES ONE 9-INCH PIE CRUST

1 ½ cups whole wheat flour

1 ½ cups quinoa flour

pinch of kosher salt

1 cup (2 sticks) cold unsalted butter, diced

¼ cup ice water

1. In a large bowl, stir together the whole wheat flour, quinoa flour, and salt. Use a pastry cutter, two knives, or your clean hands to work the butter into the flour until the mixture resembles coarse crumbs, with butter pieces about the size of peas.

2. Gradually add the ice water a tablespoon at a time, stirring with a fork until the dough comes together. Turn onto a well-floured work surface and knead two or three times, just enough for the dough to form into a ball. Press into a disk, wrap in plastic, and refrigerate for 30 minutes or until ready to use.

3. To make the crust, preheat the oven to 400°F. Spray a 9-inch pie pan with cooking spray or grease with butter. Roll the refrigerated dough into a roughly 10- or 11-inch circle on a generously floured work surface, making sure the dough doesn't stick. Transfer to the prepared pan, trim off any excess, and, if you wish, crimp the edges with your fingers or a fork for decoration. Prick the crust all over the bottom and sides with a fork, line the crust with aluminum foil, and fill the bottom of the crust with pie weights or dried beans to keep it from shrinking. Bake for about 10 minutes, remove the foil and weights, return to the oven, and continue to bake until golden, about 5 minutes longer. Fill as desired.

CHAPTER 2
Breakfasts

The recipes in this chapter reinvent all our old favorites using quinoa, from make-ahead muffins or a quick smoothie to weekend treats such as pancakes and waffles. They're an easy way to start any day with a healthy, hearty breakfast.

WINTER

Hearty Multigrain Pancakes

Quinoa Biscuits and Gravy

Quinoa Porridge with Stewed Fruits

SPRING

Banana Nut Power Muffins

Lemon-Ricotta Pancakes

Asparagus-Provolone Quiche

SUMMER

Honey-Cinnamon Granola

Savory Quinoa-Corn Griddle Cakes
with Wilted Spinach and Fried Eggs

Tri-berry Smoothie

FALL

Banana Pancakes

Pumpkin Waffles

Quinoa, Sweet Potato, and Smoked
Salmon Hash

HEARTY MULTIGRAIN PANCAKES

These are exactly what multigrain pancakes should be: chewy, dense, and hearty. Delicious with maple syrup, they would also stand up nicely to a fruit compote. This batter is a great way to use up extra cooked quinoa from another meal; skip step 1 and use about ¾ cup cooked red or white quinoa in place of the uncooked quinoa and water. **MAKES 12 TO 14 PANCAKES**

¼ cup white or red quinoa, rinsed

½ cup water

½ cup whole wheat flour

1 cup all-purpose flour

½ cup old-fashioned rolled oats

2 teaspoons baking powder

1 teaspoon baking soda

1 tablespoon brown sugar

⅛ teaspoon kosher salt

2 large eggs

1½ cups buttermilk

1 tablespoon vanilla extract

3 tablespoons unsalted butter, melted and cooled slightly

2 tablespoons flax seeds

unsalted butter, as needed

1 cup blueberries (optional)

real maple syrup

1. In a small saucepan over high heat, bring the quinoa and water to a boil. Reduce heat to low, cover, and cook until the water has been absorbed and the quinoa is tender, 10 to 12 minutes. Turn off the heat and let the quinoa sit for 5 minutes. Fluff with a fork and allow to cool slightly.

2. In a large bowl, stir together the whole wheat flour, all-purpose flour, rolled oats, baking powder, baking soda, brown sugar, and salt.

3. In a medium bowl, whisk the eggs, then whisk in the buttermilk, vanilla, and melted butter. Pour the egg mixture into the flour mixture and stir just until combined. Gently stir in the cooked quinoa and the flax seeds.

4. Heat a griddle or large nonstick skillet over medium-high heat. Add a dollop of butter and melt, spreading with a large, flat spatula or tilting to coat the skillet completely. Spoon the batter onto the griddle or skillet, about ¼ cup per pancake, and immediately sprinkle blueberries, if using, on top of each one. Cook until the underside is golden and the edges appear dry, about 7 minutes. Turn the pancakes over and cook through, 4 to 5 minutes longer. Repeat with the rest of the batter, adding more butter to the griddle or skillet as needed. Keep cooked pancakes warm in a 170°F oven while you finish cooking the rest of the batter. Serve hot with maple syrup.

QUINOA BISCUITS AND GRAVY

We love this classic Southern dish for the occasional indulgent breakfast, and we were happy to find that quinoa flour works just as well as wheat flour to make a creamy, thick gravy. Use the biscuit recipe from the Essential Recipes chapter as a base for the cheese-parsley biscuits. SERVES 4

1 recipe Quinoa Buttermilk Biscuits (page 21)

½ cup shredded cheddar cheese (about 2 ounces)

1 tablespoon chopped flat-leaf parsley

½ pound breakfast sausage links or patties

1 tablespoon unsalted butter, as needed

3 tablespoons quinoa flour

½ teaspoon dried thyme

½ teaspoon dried sage

2 cups whole milk

kosher salt and black pepper

hot sauce, such as Tabasco (optional)

1. Make the buttermilk biscuits according to the recipe instructions, stirring in the cheese and parsley along with the buttermilk in Step 3. Bake as instructed.

2. Meanwhile, remove the sausage from the casings or crumble the patties. In a large nonstick skillet over medium heat, cook the sausage until browned and cooked through, 5 to 7 minutes, using a wooden spoon or spatula to break up any large chunks. If more than about 2 tablespoons grease remains in the skillet when the sausage is cooked, tilt the skillet and spoon out the excess. If the sausage seems dry after cooking, add 1 tablespoon butter to the skillet and let it melt.

3. Sprinkle the flour over the sausage and cook over medium heat, stirring frequently, until the flour browns, 3 to 4 minutes. Stir in the thyme and sage. Gradually stir in the milk. Reduce the heat to low and simmer, stirring occasionally, until thickened, 5 to 7 minutes. Season to taste with salt, pepper, and hot sauce, if using.

4. To serve, place one or two biscuits on each plate and spoon gravy over them. Serve hot.

QUINOA PORRIDGE WITH STEWED FRUITS

Enriched with agave syrup and topped with a dollop of vanilla yogurt, this fancy porridge is one of our favorite ways to start a cold winter day. Use whatever combination of dried fruits you have on hand; our favorites are cranberries, apricots, dates, and cherries. If you don't have agave syrup, you can substitute maple syrup, honey, or even brown sugar. **SERVES 2**

½ tablespoon unsalted butter

½ cup white quinoa, rinsed

½ cup water

½ cup whole milk

2 teaspoons agave syrup

½ teaspoon vanilla extract

½ teaspoon ground cinnamon

½ cup chopped dried fruits, such as cranberries, apricots, or dates

1 tablespoon vanilla yogurt

1. In a small saucepan, melt the butter over medium heat. Add the quinoa and sauté until lightly toasted, about 5 minutes. Add the water, milk, agave syrup, vanilla, cinnamon, and fruit. Bring to a simmer, then reduce the heat to low and simmer, covered, until the quinoa is tender and the liquid has been absorbed, 10 to 15 minutes.

2. Divide the porridge into two bowls. Top each serving with a dollop of the vanilla yogurt to stir in before eating.

BANANA NUT POWER MUFFINS

Packed with fiber, protein, and potassium, these muffins are just the thing to fuel up for a busy day. They're a particularly good choice to pack in the gym bag as a snack following a run or a yoga class. **MAKES 12 MUFFINS**

TOPPING

2 tablespoons brown sugar

¼ cup quinoa flakes

1 tablespoon unsalted butter, melted

MUFFINS

1 ¼ cups white whole wheat flour

½ cup packed brown sugar

¾ cup quinoa flakes

½ teaspoon kosher salt

1 teaspoon baking soda

½ teaspoon baking powder

1 teaspoon ground cinnamon

3 ripe medium bananas

2 tablespoons low-fat vanilla or plain yogurt

1 tablespoon canola or vegetable oil

2 large eggs, beaten

1 teaspoon vanilla extract

¾ cup chopped walnuts

1. Preheat the oven to 350°F. Spray 12 cups of a standard muffin pan with cooking spray.

2. **For the Topping:** In a small bowl, combine the brown sugar, quinoa flakes, and melted butter. Stir until the butter completely coats the quinoa and brown sugar. Set aside.

3. **For the Muffins:** In a large bowl, stir together the white whole wheat flour, brown sugar, quinoa flakes, salt, baking soda, baking powder, and cinnamon.

4. In a medium bowl, mash the bananas with a fork until smooth. Add the yogurt, oil, beaten eggs, and vanilla. Stir the banana mixture into the flour mixture until just combined. Fold in the walnuts.

5. Spoon the batter evenly among the prepared muffin cups. Sprinkle with the topping mixture. Bake until the tops of the muffins are light brown and spring back when pressed lightly, 15 to 20 minutes. Cool in the pan on a wire rack for 10 minutes, then transfer the muffins directly to the wire rack to cool completely. Store at room temperature in a covered container for 1 to 2 days.

LEMON-RICOTTA PANCAKES

One of my favorite recipes from my tenure at McCall's magazine was a Lemon-Ricotta Pancake from a restaurant at The Little Nell resort hotel in Aspen. This version is sure to be met with rave reviews.—KS **MAKES 6 TO 8 PANCAKES**

PANCAKES
½ cup quinoa flour

½ cup quinoa flakes

½ teaspoon kosher salt

1 teaspoon baking powder

¾ teaspoon grated nutmeg

2 large eggs, at room temperature

⅔ cup ricotta

2 tablespoons honey

½ cup whole milk

1 teaspoon grated lemon zest

1 tablespoon fresh lemon juice

¼ teaspoon cream of tartar

unsalted butter, as needed

1 cup blackberries

HONEY WHIPPED CREAM
½ cup heavy cream

1 teaspoon vanilla extract

2 tablespoons honey

1. **For the Pancakes:** In a medium bowl, stir together the quinoa flour, quinoa flakes, salt, baking powder, and nutmeg.

2. Separate the egg whites and yolks into two medium bowls; set aside the whites. Add the ricotta, 2 tablespoons of the honey, and the milk to the egg yolks and whisk to combine. Stir the flour mixture into the yolk mixture until combined. Let rest for 5 minutes, then add the lemon zest and juice and whisk to combine.

3. Beat the egg whites with an electric mixer on low speed until they begin to foam, about 1 minute. Add the cream of tartar, increase the mixer speed to medium-high, and continue beating until firm peaks form, 1 to 2 minutes longer. Using a rubber spatula, gently fold the egg whites into the batter until just combined.

4. **For the Honey Whipped Cream:** Combine the heavy cream, vanilla, and remaining 2 tablespoons honey in a cold medium bowl. Using an electric mixer on low to medium speed, beat until firm peaks form.

5. Heat a griddle or large nonstick skillet over medium heat. Add a dollop of butter and melt, spreading with a large flat spatula or tilting to coat the skillet completely. Spoon the pancake batter onto the griddle or skillet, about ⅓ cup per pancake. Cook until the underside is golden and the edges appear dry, 5 to 7 minutes, then flip and cook through, 3 to 5 minutes longer. Repeat with the rest of the batter, adding more butter to the griddle or skillet as needed. If desired, keep cooked pancakes warm in a 170°F oven while you make the rest.

6. To serve, place 2 or 3 pancakes on each plate and top with the honey whipped cream and blackberries.

ASPARAGUS-PROVOLONE QUICHE

This classic brunch dish is elegant and refined, perfect for a holiday morning or a get-together with friends over mimosas. But don't limit it to the pre-noon hours—paired with a green salad, it's a nice lunch or light dinner. Any leftovers make for a good grab-and-go weekday breakfast. SERVES 4 TO 6

1 recipe Quinoa–Rice Flour Pie Crust (page 30)

6 large eggs

½ cup whole milk

½ cup half-and-half

½ teaspoon Dijon mustard

½ teaspoon kosher salt

pinch of black pepper

1 ¼ cups grated provolone cheese, divided (about 5 ounces)

2 cups 1-inch asparagus pieces, steamed or roasted (about 6 ounces)

2 tablespoons minced fresh chives

1. Prepare and bake the pie crust according to the recipe instructions.

2. Preheat the oven to 400°F. In a medium bowl, whisk the eggs, then whisk in the milk, half-and-half, mustard, salt, and pepper.

3. Sprinkle 1 cup of the provolone cheese over the bottom of the baked pie crust. Distribute the asparagus and the chives evenly over the cheese. Pour the egg mixture over the vegetables. Sprinkle the remaining ¼ cup cheese on top.

4. Bake until the filling is set and no longer jiggles when shaken slightly, 30 to 35 minutes. Let stand for 5 minutes before slicing. Serve warm or at room temperature.

HONEY-CINNAMON GRANOLA

Once you learn how easy it is to make your own delicious granola, you'll never buy the expensive packaged varieties again. This recipe can be customized according to your own taste. Use maple syrup in place of the honey, for instance, or substitute your favorite nuts, seeds, and dried fruit. Serve this granola over yogurt or ice cream, with milk, or just to eat out of hand. MAKES 4 CUPS

1 cup rolled oats

1 cup quinoa flakes

½ cup slivered almonds

½ cup roasted sunflower seeds

⅓ cup sweetened coconut flakes

2 tablespoons flax seeds

2 tablespoons unsalted butter

⅓ cup honey

1 teaspoon vanilla extract

1 teaspoon ground cinnamon

⅔ cup raisins or dried cranberries

1. Preheat the oven to 325°F. Line a rimmed baking sheet with parchment paper.

2. In a large bowl, combine the oats, quinoa flakes, almonds, sunflower seeds, coconut, and flax seeds.

3. Place the butter in a small microwave-safe bowl and microwave for 30 seconds at 60 percent power, repeating as needed in 10-second increments until the butter is melted. Or, melt the butter in a small saucepan over medium-low heat. Stir in the honey until the butter and honey are completely incorporated into a thick, smooth mixture. Stir in the vanilla and cinnamon. Pour the honey mixture over the oat mixture, using a spatula to coat the dry ingredients completely with the honey mixture. Turn the mixture out onto the prepared baking sheet and spread in an even layer.

4. Bake until all the ingredients are browned, 30 to 35 minutes, stirring every 10 minutes. Cool in the pan on a wire rack. When cool, sprinkle the granola with the raisins or dried cranberries, then transfer to an airtight container or zip-top plastic bag. The granola will keep for 1 to 2 weeks, getting crunchier over time if stored properly.

SAVORY QUINOA-CORN GRIDDLE CAKES WITH WILTED SPINACH AND FRIED EGGS

These quinoa-cornmeal griddle cakes are studded with kernels of corn. Topped with spinach and a fried egg, they make a substantial breakfast or brunch entrée. SERVES 4

GRIDDLE CAKES

½ cup quinoa flour

¼ cup masa harina

¼ teaspoon kosher salt

2 large eggs

¾ cup whole milk

2 tablespoons minced chives

kernels from 1 ear of corn, or 1 cup frozen corn, thawed

¼ teaspoon cream of tartar

unsalted butter, as needed

2 teaspoons extra-virgin olive oil

6 cups fresh spinach leaves (8 ounces)

1 tablespoon unsalted butter

4 large eggs

¼ cup grated Parmesan cheese

kosher salt and black pepper

1. **For the Griddle Cakes:** In a large bowl, stir together the quinoa flour, masa harina, and salt.

2. Separate the egg whites and yolks into two medium bowls; set aside the whites. Whisk the milk and chives into the egg yolks. Stir into the flour mixture until combined; stir in the corn. Set aside.

3. Beat the egg whites with an electric mixer on low speed until they begin to foam, about 1 minute. Add the cream of tartar, increase the speed to medium-high, and continue beating until firm peaks form, 1 to 2 minutes longer. Using a spatula, gently fold the egg whites into the batter until just combined.

4. Heat a griddle or large nonstick skillet over medium heat. Add a dollop of butter and melt, spreading with a large, flat spatula or tilting to coat the skillet. Spoon the batter onto the griddle or skillet, about ¼ cup per griddle cake. Cook until the underside is browned, about 5 minutes, then flip to cook through, 3 to 5 minutes longer. Repeat with the rest of the batter, adding butter to the skillet as needed. If desired, keep the cooked griddle cakes warm in a 170°F oven while you cook the rest.

5. While the griddle cakes are cooking, heat the olive oil in a large nonstick skillet over medium heat. Add the spinach and cook, turning occasionally with tongs, until wilted, 3 to 5 minutes. Season to taste with salt and pepper.

In South America, the bitter saponin that coats quinoa seeds is used as a cleanser (for both skin and clothing) and as a topical antiseptic for skin injuries.

6. When the griddle cakes are cooked, melt the butter on the griddle or skillet and break the eggs carefully onto it. Fry until the white is mostly set, 3 to 4 minutes, then carefully turn over each egg and fry until the yolk is cooked to your preferred doneness, 1 to 2 minutes more. Season lightly with salt and pepper, if desired.

7. To serve, overlap two pancakes on each of four plates. Divide the spinach among the four servings on top of the pancakes. Place an egg on top of the spinach on each plate and sprinkle with Parmesan cheese.

TRI-BERRY SMOOTHIE

This quick smoothie not only satisfies for breakfast but also makes a great snack, especially before any energy-burning activity. You can substitute almond, soy, or any other type of milk for the whole milk in this recipe. MAKES 4 (8-OUNCE) SERVINGS

⅓ cup white quinoa, rinsed

⅔ cup water

2 cups whole milk

1 cup fresh or frozen raspberries

1 cup fresh or frozen strawberries

1 cup fresh or frozen blueberries

2 tablespoons honey

1. In a small saucepan over high heat, bring the quinoa and water to a boil. Reduce the heat to low, cover, and cook until the water has been absorbed and the quinoa is tender, 10 to 12 minutes. Turn off the heat and let the quinoa sit for 5 minutes. Fluff with a fork. Turn the quinoa out onto a rimmed baking sheet, spread into an even layer, and refrigerate to cool completely.

2. Combine the cooked quinoa and the milk in the jar of a blender and purée until smooth, about 2 minutes. Add the raspberries, strawberries, blueberries, and honey; purée until smooth, 1 to 2 minutes. Thin with additional milk, as needed. Pour into 4 glasses and serve cold.

BANANA PANCAKES

*Kick-start any day with these fluffy but filling pancakes that pack a nutritional punch
of potassium. Use bananas that are very ripe and mushy, with skins that are spotted brown,
along with a firmer, less-ripe banana to dice into the batter.*   MAKES 8 TO 10 PANCAKES

½ cup quinoa flour

½ cup quinoa flakes

½ teaspoon kosher salt

1 teaspoon baking powder

3 bananas, 2 overripe and 1 ripe but firm

2 large eggs, at room temperature

½ cup whole milk

3 tablespoons real maple syrup

½ cup chopped walnuts (optional)

¼ teaspoon cream of tartar

unsalted butter, as needed

1. In a medium bowl, stir together the quinoa flour, quinoa flakes, salt, and baking powder.

2. In a second medium bowl, beat the 2 overripe bananas with an electric mixer on low speed until smooth.

3. Separate the egg whites into a third medium bowl and the yolks into the bowl with the bananas. Add the milk and maple syrup to the banana mixture and beat with an electric mixer on low speed to combine. Stir in the quinoa flour mixture and beat on low speed until combined. Dice the firm banana and use a spatula to fold the pieces, along with the walnuts, if using, into the batter. Set aside for 5 minutes.

4. Beat the egg whites with an electric mixer set on low speed until they begin to foam, about 1 minute. Add the cream of tartar, increase the speed to medium-high, and continue beating until firm peaks form, 1 to 2 minutes longer. Using a spatula, gently fold the egg whites into the batter until just combined.

5. Heat a griddle or large nonstick skillet over medium heat. Add a dollop of butter and melt, spreading the butter with a large flat spatula or tilting to coat the skillet completely. Spoon the batter onto the griddle or skillet, about ⅓ cup per pancake. Cook until the underside is golden and the edges appear dry, 5 to 7 minutes, then flip and cook through, 3 to 5 minutes longer. Repeat with the rest of the batter, adding more butter as needed. If desired, keep the cooked pancakes warm in a 170°F oven while you cook the rest.

PUMPKIN WAFFLES

Waking up to these waffles on a crisp fall morning will have you daydreaming about jumping into piles of fallen leaves. Freeze any leftover waffles and simply pop them into the toaster to reheat for a busy weekday breakfast. **MAKES 12 WAFFLES**

1 cup quinoa flour

1 cup quinoa flakes

⅓ cup packed brown sugar

1 teaspoon kosher salt

2 teaspoons baking powder

1 tablespoon pumpkin pie spice

2 large eggs

1 (15-ounce) can pure pumpkin purée

1 tablespoon molasses

1 cup whole milk

1. In a medium bowl, stir together the quinoa flour, quinoa flakes, brown sugar, salt, baking powder, and pumpkin pie spice.

2. In another medium bowl, whisk together the eggs, pumpkin purée, molasses, and milk. Stir the quinoa flour mixture into the egg mixture until combined. Set aside for 5 minutes.

3. Heat an 8-inch waffle iron on medium heat. Coat the upper and lower plates with cooking spray. Pour 1½ cups of batter into the center of the waffle iron; spread evenly with a spatula until it almost reaches the edges. Cook on medium heat for one cycle, then turn the waffle iron to high heat and cook for an additional cycle. Remove the waffle and repeat with the remaining batter. Keep warm in a 170°F oven until ready to serve.

QUINOA, SWEET POTATO, AND SMOKED SALMON HASH

Quinoa adds a nice pop to the texture of this hearty fall feast. The hash is good on its own, but you can top it with a poached farm-fresh egg and serve it with warm apple cider to make a complete meal. SERVES 4

½ cup white quinoa, rinsed

1 cup water

1 large sweet potato, peeled and cut into ½-inch cubes

1 tablespoon plus 2 teaspoons extra-virgin olive oil, divided

2 tablespoons unsalted butter

½ cup diced shallots

1 cup flaked smoked salmon

¼ cup capers

½ cup heavy cream

2 tablespoons Dijon mustard

2 tablespoons chopped fresh dill

2 tablespoons sliced green onion

kosher salt and black pepper

1. Preheat the oven to 400°F. In a small saucepan over high heat, bring the quinoa and water to a boil. Reduce the heat to low, cover, and cook until the water has been absorbed and the quinoa is tender, 10 to 12 minutes. Turn off the heat and let the quinoa sit for 5 minutes. Fluff with a fork, cover again, and leave on the stove to keep warm.

2. In a medium bowl, toss together the sweet potato, 2 teaspoons of the olive oil, and a pinch of salt. Spread onto a rimmed nonstick baking sheet and bake, stirring occasionally, until browned and fork tender, about 15 minutes. Remove from the oven and loosely cover with aluminum foil to keep warm.

3. Heat a large skillet over medium-high heat and add the remaining olive oil and the butter. Once the butter has melted, add the shallots and cook, stirring occasionally, until translucent, about 5 minutes. Add the sweet potato, quinoa, smoked salmon, and capers. Stir to combine and cook to heat through, 3 to 4 minutes.

4. In a small bowl, whisk the heavy cream and Dijon mustard to combine. Add the mixture to the skillet, stir to combine, and cook 2 minutes longer. Season to taste with salt and pepper.

5. To serve, divide the hash among four plates. Top each serving with 1½ teaspoons each of fresh dill and green onion.

CHAPTER 3
Starters

We both love cooking meals that not only meet the nutritional needs of our families but also fulfill our playful sides. Quinoa has garnered a reputation as a "serious" seed, but starters are a great opportunity to be inventive in the kitchen. Here you'll find practical standards that are staples for almost any party, such as crackers and dips, but you can also unleash your wild side with Spicy Chicken 'n' Waffles or Eggplant "Caviar" on Grilled Quinoa Polenta.

WINTER

Multigrain Crackers

Quinoa, Bacon, and Blue Cheese
    Fritters with Horseradish-Yogurt
    Sauce

White Bean Dip

Blini Crème Fraîche and Gravlax

SPRING

Hummus

Gouda and Red Pepper Tarts

Lamb Meatballs with Tangy
    Yogurt–Goat Cheese Dip

Quinoa-Crab Salad in Lettuce Cups

SUMMER

Eggplant "Caviar" on Grilled Quinoa
    Polenta

Stuffed Squash Blossoms

Vegetarian Empanadas

Thai Summer Rolls

FALL

Sesame-Quinoa Cheese Straws

Spicy Chicken 'n' Waffles

Bacon-Wrapped Dates

MULTIGRAIN CRACKERS

These crispy rustic crackers just beg to be topped with a creamy spread, such as goat cheese, flavored cream cheese, or pub cheese. For variety, try different seeds on top—roasted pumpkin seeds or sunflower seeds, white or black sesame seeds, or chia seeds. These seeds, as well as the spelt flour used in this recipe, are easily found in natural food stores or a well-stocked grocery store. This is also a good chance to experiment with fancy salts, like smoked sea salt or pink Himalayan salt; larger grains work best. **MAKES ABOUT 3 DOZEN CRACKERS**

1 cup quinoa flour

½ cup spelt flour

½ cup whole wheat flour

1 teaspoon fine sea salt

¼ cup extra-virgin olive oil

¼ cup water, or as needed

2 tablespoons flax seeds

2 tablespoons quinoa flakes

1 tablespoon flaky sea salt

1. Preheat the oven to 350°F. Line a rimmed baking sheet with parchment paper.

2. In the bowl of a food processor, place the quinoa flour, spelt flour, whole wheat flour, and salt. Pulse to combine, about 10 pulses. With the motor running, drizzle in the olive oil through the feed tube, then gradually drizzle in the water until the mixture clumps together well when you squeeze it in your hand. You might need more or less water to achieve the right texture.

3. Turn the dough out onto a well-floured surface. Working with about a third of the dough at a time, roll it into a thin rectangle, no more than ⅛ inch thick. Prick the dough all over with a knife, then use a pizza wheel or pastry cutter to cut the dough into squares, diamonds, or any size or shape you wish. Transfer the crackers to the prepared baking sheet and brush each cracker with water, then sprinkle with the flax seeds, quinoa flakes, and flake salt.

4. Bake until the crackers are hard and browned, about 20 minutes. Transfer to a wire rack and let cool completely before storing in an airtight container. The crackers will keep for 2 to 3 days.

QUINOA, BACON, AND BLUE CHEESE FRITTERS WITH HORSERADISH-YOGURT SAUCE

These addictive little fritters can be made in bite-size pieces perfect for cocktail parties, or slightly larger for plated appetizers. Their texture and flavor are reminiscent of hush puppies. Here the fritters are pan fried, but they can also be cooked in a deep-fryer at 375°F for about 3 minutes, turning them over halfway through cooking, until browned. **MAKES 2 DOZEN FRITTERS**

⅓ cup red quinoa, or a mix of red and white, rinsed

⅔ cup water

1 cup quinoa flour

½ teaspoon kosher salt

1½ teaspoons baking powder

1 large egg

¾ cup whole milk

4 slices cooked bacon, crumbled

½ cup crumbled blue cheese (3 ounces)

2 tablespoons chopped flat-leaf parsley

½ to 1 cup canola oil, as needed for frying

½ cup plain low-fat yogurt

1 tablespoon bottled horseradish

1 tablespoon minced chives

1. In a small saucepan over high heat, bring the quinoa and water to a boil. Reduce the heat to low, cover, and cook until the water has been absorbed and the quinoa is tender, 18 to 20 minutes. Turn off the heat and let the quinoa sit for 5 minutes. Fluff with a fork.

2. Preheat the oven to 200°F. In a small bowl, stir together the quinoa flour, salt, and baking powder. In another small bowl, whisk the egg, then add the milk and whisk to combine. Pour the egg mixture into the quinoa flour mixture and whisk to combine. Fold in the bacon, quinoa, blue cheese, and parsley.

3. Line a rimmed baking sheet with paper towels. Pour enough oil into a large nonstick skillet to cover the bottom by about ¼ inch. Heat the oil over medium heat until it shimmers. Test the oil's temperature by dropping in a tiny bit of batter; if it sizzles, it's hot enough. Spoon heaping teaspoons of batter into the skillet. Do not overcrowd. Fry until browned, about 3 minutes on the first side and 2 minutes on the second side. Transfer to the prepared baking sheet and repeat with the remaining batter and additional oil, as needed. Keep cooked fritters warm in a 200°F oven.

4. Stir together the yogurt, horseradish, and chives in a small bowl, and serve with the fritters for dipping. Fritters should be served hot, as soon as possible after frying.

WHITE BEAN DIP

This white bean dip, with its quinoa topping, is tasty with both crudités and crackers. For a tasty chip, try the variation of the Quinoa Tortillas recipe (page 22). MAKES 3 CUPS

DIP

1 head garlic

4 tablespoons extra-virgin olive oil, divided

⅓ cup quinoa flakes

1 cup vegetable stock or broth

1 (15-ounce) can cannellini beans, drained and rinsed

½ teaspoon minced fresh rosemary

2 tablespoons chopped flat-leaf parsley

1 teaspoon grated lemon zest

1 tablespoon fresh lemon juice

kosher salt and black pepper

TOPPING

⅓ cup white quinoa, rinsed

⅔ cup water

1 tablespoon chopped flat-leaf parsley

1 tablespoon extra-virgin olive oil

¼ teaspoon grated lemon zest

1 tablespoon fresh lemon juice

½ teaspoon kosher salt

¼ teaspoon black pepper

1. **For the Dip:** Preheat the oven to 400°F. Cut the top off of the head of garlic to expose the cloves. Place the garlic on a piece of aluminum foil and fold up the sides partway, like a small bowl. Pour 2 tablespoons of the olive oil over the garlic and close the top of the foil. Place the foil packet on a rimmed baking sheet and bake for 1 hour. Remove from the oven and allow to cool.

2. Meanwhile, cook the quinoa flakes according to the package instructions, using vegetable stock or broth in place of water. Cool and reserve.

3. Squeeze the roasted garlic cloves out of their skins into the bowl of a food processor. Add the cooked quinoa flakes and the remaining 2 tablespoons olive oil, then process until smooth, about 45 seconds. Add the cannellini beans and process until smooth, about 1 minute. Add the rosemary, parsley, and lemon zest and juice, salt, and pepper. Process until combined, about 30 seconds. Taste and adjust the seasoning with salt and pepper as needed. Transfer to a serving bowl, cover, and reserve in the refrigerator.

4. **For the Topping:** In a small saucepan over high heat, bring the quinoa and water to a boil. Reduce the heat to low, cover, and cook until the water has been absorbed and the quinoa is tender, 10 to 12 minutes. Turn off the heat and let the quinoa sit for 5 minutes. Fluff with a fork and allow to cool.

5. In a medium bowl, combine the quinoa, parsley, olive oil, and lemon zest and juice. Season to taste with salt and pepper.

6. Top the dip with the quinoa mixture to serve.

BLINI WITH CRÈME FRAÎCHE AND GRAVLAX

This recipe will quickly become your go-to for guests, since it's versatile enough to serve for brunch and a cocktail party alike. These fancy but easy blini are sure to have your guests thinking you've spent hours in the kitchen. Gravlax is salmon that has been cold-cured in salt, sugar, and spices. It is available at most specialty food stores and can even be purchased at IKEA. Tobiko can be purchased in the seafood department of most Asian and specialty food stores. MAKES 20 TO 24 BLINI

1 recipe Quinoa Buttermilk Pancakes (page 19)

1 cup whole milk

unsalted butter, as needed

6 tablespoons crème fraîche

2 pounds gravlax

4 tablespoons tobiko (flying fish roe)

24 small sprigs fresh dill

1. Make the quinoa buttermilk pancake batter according to the recipe instructions, but reduce the honey to 2 tablespoons and substitute 1 cup of milk for the buttermilk in the recipe.

2. Heat a griddle or large nonstick skillet over medium heat. Add a dollop of butter and melt, spreading with a large flat spatula or tilting to coat the skillet completely. Spoon the batter onto the griddle or skillet, about 2 tablespoons per blini. Cook until the underside is golden and little bubbles form on top, about 4 minutes, then flip and cook through, 3 to 4 minutes longer. Repeat with the rest of the batter, adding butter to the griddle or skillet as needed. Let cool.

3. To serve, top each blini with ¾ teaspoon crème fraîche, 2 ounces gravlax, ½ teaspoon tobiko, and a small sprig of fresh dill.

HUMMUS

This back-to-basics Mediterranean spread can be used as a dip or on sandwiches. Vary the recipe by adding roasted red peppers, kalamata olives, feta cheese, or almost anything you please. The quinoa flakes add a pleasing nuttiness and enhance the silky-smooth texture of the hummus. MAKES 2½ CUPS

½ cup quinoa flakes

½ cup vegetable stock or broth

1 (15-ounce) can chickpeas, drained and rinsed

2 medium cloves garlic, minced

¼ cup tahini

3 tablespoons fresh lemon juice

¼ teaspoon ground cumin

½ teaspoon kosher salt

¼ teaspoon black pepper

3 tablespoons extra-virgin olive oil, divided

¼ teaspoon paprika

1. In a small bowl, cover the quinoa flakes with the vegetable stock or broth. Let sit for 2 minutes until the flakes are softened.

2. Place the soaked quinoa flakes, the chickpeas, and the garlic in the bowl of a food processor and process until smooth, about 1 minute. Add the tahini, lemon juice, cumin, salt, pepper, and 2 tablespoons of the olive oil. Process until combined, about 45 seconds. Taste and adjust the seasoning with salt and pepper, as needed. Transfer to a serving bowl and top with the remaining 1 tablespoon olive oil and the paprika.

GOUDA AND RED PEPPER TARTS

Stir leftover cooked quinoa into these bite-size tarts to make the quiche-like filling a little denser. You'll need about ¼ to ½ cup of leftover cooked quinoa. If you make the quinoa from scratch as instructed in the recipe directions, you'll likely have a little left over to reserve for another use. To change things up further, use Quinoa Pilaf (page 28) or another seasoned variation, or substitute a different kind of cheese. MAKES ABOUT 20 (2-INCH) TARTS

½ cup white quinoa, rinsed

1 cup water

1 recipe Quinoa–Whole Wheat Pie Crust (page 31)

2 large eggs

¾ cup whole milk

¼ cup heavy cream

½ teaspoon dry mustard

¼ teaspoon salt

pinch of black pepper

¼ cup finely chopped roasted red peppers

½ cup shredded Gouda cheese (2 to 3 ounces)

1. Preheat the oven to 350°F. In a small saucepan over high heat, bring the quinoa and water to a boil. Reduce the heat to low, cover, and cook until the water has been absorbed and the quinoa is tender, 10 to 12 minutes. Turn off the heat and let the quinoa sit for 5 minutes. Fluff with a fork and allow to cool.

2. Prepare the dough for the pie crust according to the recipe instructions. Use your fingers or a tart tamper to press tablespoon-size pieces of dough into the wells of a mini tart pan (with 2-inch-diameter wells). Use a fork to prick the bottoms and sides of each tart crust to keep air bubbles from forming, and bake until browned, 10 to 15 minutes.

3. While the crust is baking, in a medium bowl whisk the eggs, then whisk in the milk, cream, mustard, salt, and pepper until smooth.

4. When the crust is baked, reduce the oven temperature to 325°F. Spoon about ½ teaspoon each of the quinoa, red peppers, and cheese into each baked tart crust. Carefully fill each tart to the top with the egg mixture.

5. Return the tarts to the oven and bake until the filling is set, about 20 minutes. Serve hot or at room temperature.

LAMB MEATBALLS WITH TANGY YOGURT–GOAT CHEESE DIP

These lamb meatballs are packed with flavor. Stuff any leftover meatballs into a whole wheat pita with lettuce, tomato, and a drizzle of the dip to make a sandwich for lunch. Or drop the dip and add the meatballs to your favorite spaghetti sauce for an updated take on a traditional favorite. **MAKES 18 TO 20 MEATBALLS**

MEATBALLS
⅓ cup white quinoa, rinsed

⅔ cup water

1½ cups ground lamb

½ cup canned chickpeas, drained, rinsed, and chopped

1 small yellow onion, minced

1 medium clove garlic, minced

¾ teaspoon ground allspice

1 tablespoon chopped fresh mint

2 tablespoons chopped flat-leaf parsley

½ teaspoon kosher salt

¼ teaspoon black pepper

DIP
1 cup plain low-fat yogurt

¼ cup goat cheese

1 teaspoon dry mustard

4 teaspoons fresh lemon juice

1 tablespoon honey

kosher salt and black pepper

1. **For the Meatballs:** In a small saucepan over high heat, bring the quinoa and water to a boil. Reduce the heat to low, cover, and cook until the water has been absorbed and the quinoa is tender, 10 to 12 minutes. Turn off the heat and let the quinoa sit for 5 minutes. Fluff with a fork and allow to cool.

2. Preheat the oven to 350°F. Spray a rimmed baking sheet with cooking spray. In a medium bowl, combine the cooked quinoa with the ground lamb, chickpeas, onion, garlic, allspice, mint, parsley, salt, and pepper. Work the ingredients together with your clean hands.

3. Using a 1-tablespoon measure, scoop the lamb mixture onto the prepared baking sheet. Roll the scooped meatballs between the palms of your hands to form balls and replace on the baking sheet. Bake for 15 minutes, turning every 5 minutes to brown on all sides and cooking to an internal temperature of 160°F. Remove from the oven and reduce the oven temperature to 170°F. Loosely cover the meatballs with aluminum foil and return to the oven to keep warm.

4. **For the Dip:** In a small bowl, combine the yogurt, goat cheese, dry mustard, lemon juice, and honey. Beat with an electric mixer on low speed until smooth. Season to taste with salt and pepper. Transfer the dip to a serving bowl and serve with the warm meatballs.

QUINOA-CRAB SALAD IN LETTUCE CUPS

With its pretty presentation and fancy ingredients, this appetizer is lovely to serve at an elegant brunch, an afternoon tea party, or a bridal shower. You can prepare the salad ahead of time, but don't cut up or add the avocado until just before serving, as avocado quickly turns brown when exposed to air.   MAKES 12 TO 16 LETTUCE CUPS

1 cup white quinoa, rinsed

2 cups water

8 ounces cooked crab meat, picked through for shells

1 avocado, pitted, peeled, and diced

2 tablespoons capers

2 tablespoons chopped fresh tarragon, plus 12 to 16 tarragon sprigs for garnish

¼ cup Champagne vinegar

1 teaspoon Dijon mustard

⅛ teaspoon sea salt

pinch of white pepper

⅓ cup extra-virgin olive oil

2 heads Bibb lettuce, separated into individual leaves

paprika, for garnish

1. In a medium saucepan over high heat, bring the quinoa and water to a boil. Reduce the heat to low, cover, and cook until the water has been absorbed and the quinoa is tender, 10 to 12 minutes. Turn off the heat and let the quinoa sit for 5 minutes. Fluff with a fork and allow to cool to room temperature.

2. In a large bowl, combine the quinoa, crab meat, avocado, capers, and tarragon.

3. In a small bowl, whisk together the vinegar, mustard, salt, and pepper. Continue whisking and gradually drizzle in the olive oil until the mixture is smooth. Drizzle over the quinoa mixture and stir gently to coat.

4. Just before serving, arrange the lettuce cups on a platter or place on individual salad plates. Spoon ¼ to ⅓ cup of the quinoa-crab salad into each lettuce cup. Sprinkle with paprika and top each serving with a sprig of tarragon.

EGGPLANT "CAVIAR" ON GRILLED QUINOA POLENTA

This elegant appetizer is far easier to prepare than it looks. The eggplant mixture can be made a day or two ahead and reheated to serve on ready-made quinoa polenta (the kind that comes in a tube)—just slice and grill! **MAKES 10 APPETIZERS**

1 medium eggplant

1 tablespoon plus 1 teaspoon extra-virgin olive oil, divided

1 teaspoon fresh lemon juice

1 (18-ounce) package prepared quinoa polenta, any flavor, chilled in the refrigerator

1 tablespoon canola oil

flat-leaf parsley sprigs for garnish

kosher salt and black pepper

1. Preheat the oven to 375°F. Line a rimmed baking sheet with parchment paper.

2. Cut the eggplant in half lengthwise. Brush the cut sides with 1 tablespoon of the olive oil and sprinkle with salt and pepper. Place cut-side-down on the prepared baking sheet. Bake until the eggplant is soft and can easily be pricked with a fork, about 40 minutes. Allow to cool.

3. Use a spoon to scoop the eggplant flesh away from the skin onto a cutting board. Chop with a knife until pulpy. Transfer to a bowl and add the lemon juice and the remaining 1 teaspoon olive oil. Season to taste with salt and pepper. The eggplant can be refrigerated, covered, for up to 3 days. Warm it in the microwave or in a small saucepan on the stove before serving.

4. To serve, slice the polenta into about 10 half-inch rounds. Heat a grill pan or a countertop grill to medium-high and brush the surface lightly with the canola oil. Grill the polenta rounds until grill marks appear, 3 to 4 minutes per side. Transfer to a platter and top each with about 1 tablespoon of the warm eggplant caviar. Garnish with sprigs of parsley and serve warm.

STUFFED SQUASH BLOSSOMS

Prolific garden producers, zucchini plants provide a wealth of wares for the kitchen. We recommend using male blossoms for this recipe, since they are for pollination purposes only and will not produce squash. The simplest way to differentiate male from female blossoms is the females' thicker stems. In addition, female blossoms have a small knob at the stem base, which will become the squash. Be sure to leave some male blossoms on each plant so the plants will continue to produce. Squash blossoms are also readily available at farmers' markets or specialty produce departments; look for them in mid-summer. MAKES 16 BLOSSOMS

⅓ cup tri-colored quinoa, rinsed

⅔ cup water

16 male squash blossoms

2 tablespoons extra-virgin olive oil

1 medium clove garlic, minced

1 small zucchini, shredded

2 teaspoons fresh lemon juice

⅓ cup ricotta

⅓ cup grated Parmesan cheese (about 1 ounce)

2 teaspoons chopped flat-leaf parsley

¼ teaspoon red pepper flakes (optional)

kosher salt and black pepper

canola oil, as needed for frying

1½ cups (3 recipes) Quinoa Frying Batter (page 25)

1. In a small saucepan over high heat, bring the quinoa and water to a boil. Reduce the heat to low, cover, and cook until the water has been absorbed and the quinoa is tender, 10 to 12 minutes. Turn off the heat and let the quinoa sit for 5 minutes. Fluff with a fork and allow to cool. Measure ½ cup cooked quinoa into a medium bowl and reserve the remaining quinoa for another use.

2. Gently rinse the squash blossoms in cool water. Cut an opening down one of the ribs on each flower. Remove the stamen and cut the stems to 1 inch.

3. Preheat the olive oil in a large nonstick skillet over high heat. Add the garlic and zucchini and cook, stirring occasionally, until the zucchini begins to brown, 1 to 2 minutes. Remove from the heat.

4. To the bowl with the ½ cup cooked quinoa, add the lemon juice, ricotta, Parmesan cheese, parsley, and red pepper flakes, if using. Stir to combine. Fold in the zucchini mixture. Season to taste with salt and pepper.

5. Carefully stuff each blossom with about 1 tablespoon filling. Close the opening, securing with a toothpick as needed, and twist the ends of the blossom to seal. Place on a baking sheet or a plate and refrigerate while you assemble the frying batter.

6. Fill a heavy pot, such as a Dutch oven, with canola oil to a depth of 4 to 6 inches. Heat the oil to 350°F. Line a rimmed baking sheet with paper towels. Make the frying batter according to the recipe instructions, tripling the original amounts.

7. Remove the blossoms from the refrigerator. Working in batches of 4 blossoms, hold the 1-inch stem and dredge the stuffed blossom in the frying batter to coat. Gently add the blossoms to the heated oil and cook, turning occasionally with tongs, until golden brown on all sides, 1½ to 2 minutes total. Using a slotted spoon, remove the blossoms from the oil and drain on the prepared baking sheet. Season to taste with salt. Repeat with the remaining blossoms. Serve immediately.

VEGETARIAN EMPANADAS

Serve your favorite salsa as a dipping sauce for these delectable empanadas. This recipe makes 8 medium empanadas, but you can make 16 smaller empanadas by simply dividing the tortilla dough into 16 tortillas and filling each with just ¼ cup of the black bean mixture. Make it a fiesta by serving these with traditional-style or refreshing watermelon margaritas. **MAKES 8 EMPANADAS**

⅓ cup white quinoa, rinsed

⅔ cup vegetable stock or broth

1 recipe Quinoa Tortillas (page 22)

2 tablespoons olive oil

1 small yellow onion, chopped

2 medium cloves garlic, minced

1 teaspoon dried oregano, crushed

3 tablespoons chili powder

4 cups chopped kale (1 pound)

1 (15-ounce) can black beans, drained and rinsed

kernels from 1 ear corn, or 1 cup frozen corn, thawed

1 tablespoon fresh lime juice

2 tablespoons chopped fresh cilantro

kosher salt and black pepper

1. In a small saucepan over high heat, bring the quinoa and vegetable stock or broth to a boil. Reduce the heat to low, cover, and cook until the liquid has been absorbed and the quinoa is tender, 10 to 12 minutes. Turn off the heat and let the quinoa sit for 5 minutes. Fluff with a fork and allow to cool.

2. Make the tortilla dough through Step 3 of the recipe instructions.

3. Heat the olive oil in nonstick skillet over medium-high heat. Cook the onion, stirring occasionally, until translucent, 5 to 7 minutes. Add the garlic and cook, stirring constantly, about 30 seconds. Add the oregano and chili powder and stir to combine. Add the kale and stir to combine. Cook until the kale begins to wilt, 3 to 4 minutes. Add the black beans and corn, and cook until heated through, 4 to 5 minutes. Remove from the heat, add the lime juice and cilantro, and stir to combine. Season to taste with salt and pepper.

4. Preheat the oven to 350°F. Line a rimmed baking sheet with parchment paper.

5. Roll the pieces of dough into small balls and flatten each ball into a disk. Place a sheet of waxed paper on the bottom of a tortilla press; add one disk of dough to the press and cover with another sheet of waxed paper; lower the top of the press and apply firm pressure to flatten the dough; lift the top of the press and remove the top piece of waxed paper. Gently lift the tortilla off of the press using the bottom piece of waxed paper. Repeat with the remaining dough.

6. Lay out a tortilla on a well-floured surface and add about ½ cup filling to half of the tortilla. Fold the other half over the filling and press the edges with a fork to seal. Repeat for the remaining tortillas. Place the empanadas 1 inch apart on the prepared baking sheet. Bake until golden brown, about 25 minutes.

THAI SUMMER ROLLS

This light appetizer is a refreshing summer treat. If desired, cooked prawns make a nice addition to the wrap. Should you have leftover sauce, marinate cubed chicken in the mango sauce; skewer the marinated chicken and grill to an internal temperature of 165°F. Serve with the peanut sauce for a tasty chicken satay. **MAKES 8 ROLLS**

⅓ cup white quinoa, rinsed

⅔ cup water

1 small cucumber, seeded and cut into matchsticks

1 medium carrot, peeled and cut into matchsticks

8 spring roll skins (7-inch size)

8 small green lettuce leaves

1 small ripe mango, peeled and sliced

8 sprigs fresh cilantro

8 sprigs fresh mint

MANGO SAUCE

2 cups mango nectar

1-inch piece fresh ginger, peeled and chopped

1 teaspoon hot sauce, such as Sriracha (optional)

PEANUT SAUCE

½ cup creamy peanut butter

⅔ cup light coconut milk

1 teaspoon soy sauce

½ teaspoon hot sauce, such as Sriracha (optional)

½ teaspoon fish sauce

½ teaspoon minced fresh ginger

1. In a small saucepan over high heat, bring the quinoa and water to a boil. Reduce the heat to low, cover, and cook until the water has been absorbed and the quinoa is tender, 10 to 12 minutes. Turn off the heat and let the quinoa sit for 5 minutes. Fluff with a fork and allow to cool.

2. **For the Mango Sauce:** In a medium saucepan over medium-high heat, bring the mango nectar and ginger to a boil. Reduce the heat to low and simmer until the nectar is reduced by half. Remove from the heat and strain through a fine mesh strainer into a small bowl. Stir in the hot sauce, if using. Cool and reserve.

3. **For the Peanut Sauce:** Combine all the ingredients in a medium bowl and beat with an electric mixer on low to medium speed until smooth. Reserve.

4. Prepare the spring roll skins according to the package instructions. Mix ¼ cup of the mango sauce with the cooked quinoa. Divide the cucumber and carrot matchsticks into 8 equal bundles. Gently lay out a spring roll skin; place a lettuce leaf on top, and on top of the lettuce add 2 tablespoons quinoa, 1 or 2 mango slices, 1 bundle of cucumber and carrot matchsticks, 1 sprig cilantro, and 1 sprig mint. Fold in the sides of the spring roll skin to cover the sides of the lettuce leaf; carefully fold the bottom third of the skin over the lettuce leaf and roll to close the wrap. Repeat with the remaining skins.

5. Serve the wraps with the mango and peanut dipping sauces.

SESAME-QUINOA CHEESE STRAWS

In the South, cheese straws are ubiquitous at celebrations, from weddings to birthday parties. Rich in cheese and butter, with a kick of cayenne, this version is a little softer than the manufactured kind but no less flavorful. **MAKES ABOUT 8 DOZEN STRAWS**

1¾ cups quinoa flour

1 teaspoon baking powder

1 teaspoon kosher salt

1 teaspoon dry mustard

¼ teaspoon cayenne pepper

½ cup (1 stick) unsalted butter, softened

2 cups shredded sharp cheddar cheese (about 8 ounces), at room temperature

¼ cup whole milk, or as needed

¼ cup sesame seeds

1. Preheat the oven to 375°F. Line a rimmed baking sheet with parchment paper.

2. In a medium bowl, stir together the quinoa flour, baking powder, salt, mustard, and cayenne pepper. In the bowl of a stand mixer fitted with the paddle attachment, combine the butter and the cheese, mixing at low speed until the butter is soft and the cheese is mixed in well. Gradually add the flour mixture and mix at low speed until crumbly. Add the milk and mix at low speed, increasing to medium, until the dough comes together in a ball, using a little more milk if the dough seems too crumbly.

3. You can form the straws by using a cookie press, by rolling out the dough on a floured surface to about ¼ inch thick and cutting it into thin strips, or by hand-rolling small pieces of dough into thin straws. Place the sesame seeds in a shallow dish and press each cheese straw into the seeds. Arrange the straws on the prepared baking sheet and bake until the edges are browned, 12 to 16 minutes. Cool completely on a wire rack before storing in an airtight container for up to 3 or 4 days.

SPICY CHICKEN 'N' WAFFLES

Chicken 'n' waffles combines family favorites for breakfast and dinner into a single dish. Popular from Harlem to Los Angeles, this savory and sweet combination can serve as either an hors d'oeuvre or a full meal. Substitute honey or maple syrup for the hot sauce to give this recipe a mild makeover. **SERVES 8**

16 chicken tenders (about 1 pound)

2 cups buttermilk

1 recipe Quinoa Buttermilk Pancakes (page 19)

canola oil, as needed for frying

1½ cups hot sauce, such as Frank's RedHot

1 cup quinoa flour

1 cup quinoa flakes

1½ teaspoons dry mustard

½ teaspoon garlic powder

2 tablespoons smoked paprika

½ teaspoon kosher salt

¼ teaspoon pepper

½ cup real maple syrup

1. In a medium bowl, toss the chicken tenders with the buttermilk to coat. Refrigerate for at least 2 hours or up to 24 hours, turning the chicken periodically.

2. Make the pancakes according to the recipe instructions, but make the following modifications: In Step 2, do not separate the egg yolks and whites; simply combine the eggs, honey, and buttermilk. Omit Step 3. In Step 4, instead of cooking the batter on the griddle, heat an 8-inch waffle iron to medium and coat the plates with cooking spray. Pour 1 to 1½ cups of batter into the center of the waffle iron; spread evenly with a spatula until it almost reaches the edges. Cook on medium heat for one cycle, then turn to high and cook for an additional cycle. Remove from the waffle iron and repeat with the remaining batter. Keep the waffles warm in a 170°F oven until ready to serve. (The recipe should yield about 2 waffles).

3. Fill a large heavy pot, such as a Dutch oven, with oil to a depth of 4 to 6 inches. Heat the oil to 350°F for frying. Line a rimmed baking sheet with paper towels. Pour the hot sauce into a medium bowl. Remove the chicken from the buttermilk and add it to the hot sauce. Soak for 1 to 2 minutes.

4. In a large zip-top plastic bag, combine the quinoa flour, quinoa flakes, mustard, garlic powder, paprika, salt, and pepper. Shake to combine. Add the chicken a few pieces at a time and shake to coat completely. Repeat with the remaining chicken.

5. Carefully place the chicken a few pieces at a time
into the hot oil and cook, turning occasionally with
tongs to brown evenly on all sides, 2 to 3 minutes total.
(The internal temperature of the chicken should be
165°F.) Using a slotted spoon, remove from the oil and
drain on the prepared baking sheet. Repeat with the
remaining chicken.

6. To serve, break the waffles into quarters and place
each quarter on a serving plate. Top each serving with
2 chicken tenders and drizzle with 1 tablespoon maple
syrup. Serve hot.

BACON-WRAPPED DATES

With a winning combination of savory and sweet flavors, these bite-size packages are sure to please. Red quinoa adds a nutty flavor to the filling, contrasting the sweetness of the raisins and apricots, while bacon complements the candied quality of the dates. MAKES 16

⅓ cup red quinoa, rinsed

⅔ cup water

8 slices bacon, cut in half lengthwise

4 tablespoons orange juice

2 tablespoons golden raisins

2 tablespoons minced dried apricots

¼ teaspoon ground cardamom

4 ounces goat cheese

16 large pitted dates

1. In a small saucepan over high heat, bring the quinoa and water to a boil. Reduce the heat to low, cover, and cook until the water has been absorbed and the quinoa is tender, 18 to 20 minutes. Turn off the heat and let the quinoa sit for 5 minutes. Fluff with a fork and allow to cool. Measure ½ cup cooked quinoa into a medium bowl and reserve the rest for another use.

2. While you heat a large nonstick skillet over medium heat, line a plate with paper towels. Slowly cook the bacon in the skillet, without turning it, until browned but not crisp on the underside. The bacon should be pliable enough to wrap around the dates without breaking or crumbling. Remove and drain on the prepared plate. Let cool.

3. Preheat the oven to 350°F. In a small bowl, combine the orange juice and raisins. Let soak for 10 minutes to plump the raisins.

4. Strain the orange juice into a small bowl. Add the raisins, apricots, and cardamom to the ½ cup cooked quinoa and stir to combine. Place the goat cheese in a medium bowl, add 1 tablespoon of the orange juice, and beat with an electric mixer on low speed until smooth, about 1 minute. Stir into the quinoa mixture to combine.

5. Stuff each date with about 1 tablespoon of filling. Wrap a slice of bacon around each date, with the uncooked side facing outward. Secure with a toothpick and place on a rimmed baking sheet. Bake until the bacon has browned and is crisp, 15 to 20 minutes. Remove from the oven. Cool for at least 10 minutes and remove the toothpicks before serving.

CHAPTER 4
Salads

Here, we bring you a selection of salads that appeal as both starters and sides and make perfect potluck picks, like Quinoa Caprese Salad, or try one of these recipes, like Goat Cheese Salad, at your next intimate dinner for two.

WINTER

Green Mango Salad

Grapefruit, Pomegranate, Avocado, and
    Black Quinoa Salad

Spicy Tropical Fruit Salad

SPRING

Tabouleh Salad

Goat Cheese Salad

Kimchi-Quinoa Salad

SUMMER

Fried Green Tomato Salad

Quinoa Caprese Salad

Black Bean, Corn, and Quinoa Salad
    with Lime Dressing

Lebanese "Mackashoon" Salad

FALL

Quinoa Salad with Kale, Pine Nuts, and
    Parmesan

Pickled Beet, Orange, and Quinoa
    Salad

Turkey "Waldorf" Salad

GREEN MANGO SALAD

This side dish is suited for winter, when the available mangos are often very under-ripe, but it's light enough to be served in the summer months, too. Add cooked tofu, shrimp, or chicken if you wish. SERVES 4 TO 6

½ cup black quinoa, rinsed

1 cup water

1 medium green mango, peeled and cut into matchsticks

1 medium carrot, peeled and cut into matchsticks

1 medium red bell pepper, cut into matchsticks

3 green onions, sliced (about ¼ cup)

½ cup chopped roasted cashews

¼ cup chopped fresh cilantro

¼ cup sweet chili sauce

1 tablespoon minced fresh ginger

2 teaspoons soy sauce

2½ tablespoons fresh lime juice

kosher salt

1. In a small saucepan over high heat, bring the quinoa and water to a boil. Reduce the heat to low, cover, and cook until the water has been absorbed and the quinoa is tender, 18 to 20 minutes. Turn off the heat and let the quinoa sit for 5 minutes. Fluff with a fork and allow to cool in the refrigerator.

2. In a large bowl, stir together the mango, carrot, bell pepper, green onion, cashews, cilantro, and cooked quinoa.

3. In a medium bowl, whisk together the sweet chili sauce, ginger, soy sauce, and lime juice. Add to the quinoa mixture and stir to combine. Season to taste with salt. Refrigerate for at least 1 hour and serve cold.

GRAPEFRUIT, POMEGRANATE, AVOCADO, AND BLACK QUINOA SALAD

The vibrant colors of this salad really pop against the black quinoa, making for a gorgeous presentation. **SERVES 6 TO 8**

⅔ cup black quinoa, rinsed

1⅓ cups water

1 large grapefruit, segmented, juice reserved (see sidebar)

1 teaspoon honey

1 teaspoon Campari

2 tablespoons extra-virgin olive oil

1¼ cups pomegranate seeds

1 tablespoon minced fresh mint

1 avocado, pitted, peeled, and diced

kosher salt and black pepper

1. In a medium saucepan over high heat, bring the quinoa and water to a boil. Reduce the heat to low, cover, and cook until the water has been absorbed and the quinoa is tender, 18 to 20 minutes. Turn off the heat and let the quinoa sit for 5 minutes. Fluff with a fork and allow to cool.

2. Place the grapefruit segments in a medium bowl. In a small bowl, whisk together the grapefruit juice, honey, and Campari. Slowly add the olive oil while continually whisking to emulsify the dressing. Season with a pinch of kosher salt.

3. Add the cooked quinoa, pomegranate seeds, and dressing to the grapefruit slices, and stir to combine. Using a rubber spatula, fold in the mint and avocado. Season to taste with additional salt and pepper, as needed. Serve chilled or at room temperature.

TO SEGMENT CITRUS FRUIT

Use a serrated knife to cut the top and bottom off the fruit, just exposing the flesh. Place the fruit with one of the flat sides resting on your work surface and follow the curve of the side from top to bottom to slice off the peel where the pith and the flesh meet. Working over a bowl to catch the juice, use a sharp paring knife to carefully cut along the membrane to free the segments. After all the segments have been removed, squeeze the remaining juice from the peel and membranes.

SPICY TROPICAL FRUIT SALAD

The spice in this salad plays nicely off of the sweetness of the fresh and dried fruits.
Eliminate the rum to make this dish kid friendly. This salad pairs well with grilled chicken
or fish and roasted pork. **SERVES 4 TO 6**

1 cup white quinoa, rinsed

2 cups water

2 medium oranges, segmented, juice reserved (see page 67)

2 tablespoons diced dried apricots

2 tablespoons golden raisins

¼ cup chopped dates

½ cup chopped dried pineapple

⅓ cup chopped hazelnuts

1 cup cubed jicama

1 small banana, peeled and chopped

2 tablespoons frozen pineapple juice concentrate, thawed

2 tablespoons honey

1 tablespoon spiced rum

1 teaspoon chili powder

¼ cup extra-virgin olive oil

kosher salt and black pepper

¼ cup diced fresh herbs, such as chives, mint, or basil (optional)

1. In a medium saucepan over high heat, bring the quinoa and water to a boil. Reduce the heat to low, cover, and cook until the water has been absorbed and the quinoa is tender, 10 to 12 minutes. Turn off heat and let the quinoa sit for 5 minutes. Fluff with a fork and allow to cool.

2. Place the orange segments in a medium bowl and the orange juice in a small bowl. In the medium bowl add the quinoa, dried apricots, raisins, dates, dried pineapple, hazelnuts, jicama, and banana, and stir to combine.

3. In the small bowl with the orange juice, add the pineapple juice concentrate, honey, spiced rum, and chili powder, and whisk to combine. Slowly add the olive oil while continually whisking to emulsify the dressing. Add the dressing to the quinoa mixture, stirring to combine. Season to taste with salt and pepper. Refrigerate until cold. Just before serving, garnish with fresh herbs if desired.

TABOULEH SALAD

A staple of Middle Eastern cuisine, this salad is a natural use for quinoa. Substitute red quinoa to add a nutty quality to the salad, or use black quinoa for a great contrast of color. This recipe is a simple solution for picnics.   **SERVES 6 TO 8**

⅔ cup white quinoa, rinsed

1⅓ cups water

1 cup halved cherry tomatoes

1 small cucumber, seeded and diced

½ cup canned chickpeas, drained and rinsed

2 tablespoons sliced green onion

¼ cup chopped flat-leaf parsley

2 tablespoons chopped fresh mint

½ teaspoon ground allspice

2 tablespoons fresh lemon juice

¼ cup extra-virgin olive oil

kosher salt and black pepper

1. In a medium saucepan over high heat, bring the quinoa and water to a boil. Reduce the heat to low, cover, and cook until the water has been absorbed and the quinoa is tender, 10 to 12 minutes. Turn off the heat and let the quinoa sit for 5 minutes. Fluff with a fork and allow to cool.

2. In a large bowl, stir together the cooked quinoa, cherry tomatoes, cucumber, chickpeas, green onion, parsley, mint, allspice, lemon juice, and olive oil. Season to taste with salt and pepper. Cover and refrigerate for at least 1 hour before serving so the flavors can marry. Serve cold or at room temperature.

GOAT CHEESE SALAD

This is a great goat-to recipe for company. Need we say more?　Serves 4

¾ cup extra-virgin olive oil

2 tablespoons chopped flat-leaf parsley, divided

½ teaspoon minced fresh rosemary

½ teaspoon fresh thyme leaves

½ teaspoon red pepper flakes (optional)

1 (4-ounce) log goat cheese, cut into 4 rounds

¼ cup balsamic vinegar

1 tablespoon Dijon mustard

½ cup quinoa flakes

½ cup (1 recipe) Quinoa Frying Batter (page 25)

½ to 1 cup canola oil, as needed for frying

6 cups (8 ounces) fresh spinach leaves

2 cups cored and quartered strawberries (about 1 pint)

½ cup chopped hazelnuts

kosher salt and black pepper

1. In a medium bowl, combine the olive oil, 1 tablespoon parsley, rosemary, thyme, and red pepper flakes, if using. Season to taste with salt and pepper, and stir to combine. Add the goat cheese slices and submerge them in the olive oil. Cover the bowl with plastic wrap and refrigerate for 2 to 4 hours.

2. In a small bowl, whisk the vinegar and mustard to combine. Remove the goat cheese from the marinade, and strain the marinade through a fine mesh sieve into the bowl with the vinegar and mustard, whisking constantly to emulsify the dressing. Adjust the seasoning to taste with salt and pepper. Reserve.

3. In another small bowl, combine the quinoa flakes and the remaining 1 tablespoon parsley. Season with a pinch each of salt and pepper. Make the frying batter according to the recipe instructions.

4. Line a rimmed baking sheet with paper towels. Pour enough canola oil into a large nonstick skillet to cover by about ¼ inch. Heat over medium heat until it shimmers. To test the oil temperature, drop in a tiny bit of the frying batter; if it sizzles, the oil is hot enough. Dredge each goat cheese round in the batter and coat with the quinoa flake mixture. Add the goat cheese to the hot oil and cook until the bottom is golden brown, 1½ to 2 minutes, then flip and cook the second side until golden brown, 1 to 1½ minutes longer. Remove from the skillet and drain on the prepared baking sheet. Season with salt and pepper. Cover loosely with aluminum foil until ready to serve.

5. To serve, place 1½ cups of spinach on each of four plates. Top each serving with ½ cup strawberries, 1 tablespoon hazelnuts, and 1 fried goat cheese round. Drizzle dressing over the top of each salad.

KIMCHI-QUINOA SALAD

A spicy Korean dish made with napa cabbage, kimchi can be an acquired taste—it's usually spicier than many people are accustomed to eating. Prepared kimchi can be found in most Asian grocery stores. **SERVES 4 TO 6**

⅔ cup black quinoa, rinsed

1⅓ cup water

1 tablespoon minced fresh ginger

½ teaspoon sesame oil

1 tablespoon soy sauce

1 small cucumber, seeded and chopped

1 cup kimchi

1. In a medium saucepan over high heat, bring the quinoa and water to a boil. Reduce the heat to low, cover, and cook until the water has been absorbed and the quinoa is tender, 18 to 20 minutes. Turn off the heat and let the quinoa sit for 5 minutes. Fluff with a fork and allow to cool.

2. In a medium bowl, stir together the ginger, sesame oil, and soy sauce. Add the cooked quinoa, the cucumber, and the kimchi, and stir to combine. Refrigerate for at least 1 hour. Serve cold.

FRIED GREEN TOMATO SALAD

I tasted my first fried green tomato during a summer trip to Atlanta. I returned home and quickly harvested the remaining unripe tomatoes from my vines and served this salad with dinner. Next year, I may dedicate a few tomato plants to green tomatoes.—KS   **SERVES 4**

4 slices bacon

2 medium oranges, segmented, juice reserved (see page 67)

1 teaspoon Champagne vinegar

2 teaspoons honey

2 teaspoons Dijon mustard

½ teaspoon minced shallots

1 teaspoon minced fresh tarragon

¼ cup extra-virgin olive oil

canola oil, as needed for frying

2 large green tomatoes

1 cup (2 recipes) Quinoa Frying Batter (page 25)

6 cups mixed baby greens

kosher salt and black pepper

1. Heat a medium nonstick skillet over medium-high heat, and cook the bacon until browned and crisp on both sides. Remove from the skillet and drain on a paper towel–lined plate. Reserve.

2. Place the orange segments in a medium bowl and 2 tablespoons of the reserved orange juice in a small bowl (discard the remaining orange juice). Whisk the vinegar, honey, and mustard into the orange juice. Add the shallots and tarragon, and whisk to combine. Slowly add the olive oil, whisking continuously to emulsify the dressing. Season with a pinch of salt and pepper. Reserve.

3. Fill a large heavy pot, such as a Dutch oven, with canola oil to a depth of 4 inches. Heat the oil to 350°F for frying. Line a rimmed baking sheet with paper towels. Slice off opposite sides of the tomatoes and the stems and discard. Evenly slice each tomato into 4 slices.

4. Make the frying batter according to the recipe instructions. Working with 2 slices at a time, dip the tomatoes in the batter and carefully add them to the heated oil. Cook until the bottom is golden brown, 1½ to 2 minutes, then turn the slices over using tongs and cook the second side until golden brown, about 1 minute longer. Remove from the oil and drain on the prepared baking sheet. Season to taste with salt and pepper. Repeat with the remaining tomato slices. Keep warm in a 170°F oven until ready to serve.

5. To serve, place 1½ cups of the baby greens on each of four plates. Add a quarter of the orange segments, a crumbled slice of bacon, and 2 slices of fried green tomato. Drizzle each salad with dressing and season with additional salt and pepper as desired.

QUINOA CAPRESE SALAD

The summery, refreshing flavors of ripe tomatoes, fresh basil, and tangy balsamic vinegar combine in this twist on a classic Italian salad. Serve it chilled or at room temperature, alongside grilled meat, burgers, or a deli sandwich. If you can find ciliegini, *tiny balls of fresh mozzarella, they work great in this salad, cut in halves or quarters.* **SERVES 4**

1 cup white quinoa, rinsed

2 cups water

½ teaspoon Dijon mustard

2 tablespoons balsamic vinegar

1 tablespoon extra-virgin olive oil

3 medium tomatoes, seeded and diced

8 ounces fresh mozzarella, cut into bite-size pieces

¼ cup shredded fresh basil

2 tablespoons chopped capers

sea salt and black pepper

1. In a medium saucepan over high heat, bring the quinoa and water to a boil. Reduce the heat to low, cover, and cook until the water has been absorbed and the quinoa is tender, 10 to 12 minutes. Turn off the heat and let the quinoa sit for 5 minutes. Fluff with a fork and allow to cool.

2. Meanwhile, in a small bowl, whisk together the mustard, vinegar, and a pinch of salt. Slowly add the olive oil while whisking continuously to emulsify the dressing. Reserve.

3. When the quinoa is cool, stir in the tomatoes, mozzarella, basil, and capers. Drizzle with the dressing and toss to combine. Season to taste with pepper and more salt as desired. Serve cold or at room temperature.

BLACK BEAN, CORN, AND QUINOA SALAD WITH LIME DRESSING

This easy salad is always a hit at potlucks or casual dinner parties. It's also a great accompaniment to fajitas made on the grill. **SERVES 6 TO 8**

1 cup quinoa, rinsed

2 cups water

1 (15-ounce) can black beans, drained and rinsed

1 cup yellow corn, either fresh or frozen and thawed

1 green onion, white and green parts, sliced

2 tablespoons fresh lime juice

½ teaspoon ground cumin

½ teaspoon prepared yellow mustard

pinch of kosher salt

pinch of black pepper

pinch of granulated sugar

2 tablespoons extra-virgin olive oil

¼ cup chopped fresh cilantro

1. In a medium saucepan over high heat, bring the quinoa and water to a boil. Reduce the heat to low, cover, and cook until the water has been absorbed and the quinoa is tender, 10 to 12 minutes. Turn off the heat and let the quinoa sit for 5 minutes. Fluff with a fork and allow to cool.

2. In a medium bowl, combine the cooked quinoa, black beans, corn, and onion. In a small bowl, whisk together the lime juice, cumin, mustard, salt, pepper, and sugar. Slowly add the olive oil, whisking continuously to emulsify the dressing.

3. Drizzle the lime dressing over the quinoa mixture, stirring gently to combine. Sprinkle with the cilantro and stir to combine. Serve at room temperature or refrigerate for 2 to 3 hours to serve chilled. Stir just before serving to fluff the salad and break up any clumps.

LEBANESE "MACKASHOON" SALAD

My friend Caelyn, who is of Lebanese descent, started using quinoa in place of other grains when she learned of its health benefits; she uses it in this bright-tasting salad, for example, traditionally made with bulgur wheat. Caelyn says the salad got its name because she and a band of mischievous cousins have been dubbed the Mackashoons—a Lebanese word that loosely translates as "troublemakers." She brings this dish to her family's annual "LeboFest," a family get-together at which everyone shares something Lebanese.—JH   SERVES 4 TO 6

1 cup white quinoa, rinsed

1¾ cups water

¾ cup fresh lemon juice, divided

3 large tomatoes (such as beefsteak), coarsely chopped

1 cup coarsely chopped pitted cured black olives

1 medium onion, diced

1 cup crumbled feta cheese (about 6 ounces)

2 cloves garlic, minced

¼ cup fresh mint or 2 tablespoons dried crushed mint

½ cup extra-virgin olive oil

kosher salt and black pepper

1. In a medium saucepan, bring the quinoa, water, and ¼ cup of the lemon juice to a boil over high heat. Reduce the heat to low, cover, and cook until the water has been absorbed and the quinoa is tender, 10 to 12 minutes. Turn off the heat and let the quinoa sit for 5 minutes. Fluff with a fork, transfer to a large serving bowl, and let cool to room temperature, fluffing occasionally with a fork or spoon to speed the cooling.

2. Once the quinoa has cooled, stir in the tomatoes, olives, onion, feta cheese, garlic, and mint. In a small bowl, whisk together the remaining ½ cup lemon juice and the olive oil. Drizzle over the quinoa mixture. Season to taste with salt and pepper. Serve at room temperature, or refrigerate for up to a day and serve cold.

QUINOA SALAD WITH KALE, PINE NUTS, AND PARMESAN

We love the way Dijon mustard enhances the similarly assertive flavor of the kale, while mellow pine nuts and Parmesan cheese balance it out. You can make this salad a day ahead; the flavors develop and deepen with a little extra time in the fridge. It's also delicious served warm or at room temperature. **SERVES 6 TO 8**

4 tablespoons extra-virgin olive oil, divided

1 small onion, minced

2 cups white quinoa, rinsed

1½ cups water

3 cups chopped kale (about 12 ounces)

⅓ cup red wine vinegar

1 teaspoon Dijon mustard

½ cup toasted pine nuts

½ cup grated Parmesan cheese (about 1½ ounces)

kosher salt and black pepper

1. In a medium saucepan, heat 1 tablespoon olive oil over medium heat. Add the onion and sauté, stirring frequently, until translucent, about 5 minutes. Add the quinoa and sauté, stirring, until lightly toasted, 2 to 3 minutes. Add the water and kale, stirring to combine. Bring to a simmer, then reduce the heat to low and simmer, covered, until the quinoa is tender and the water has been absorbed, 15 to 18 minutes. Transfer the mixture to a large bowl and let cool. Stir occasionally to bring the warmer part of the mixture up from the bottom.

2. In a small bowl, whisk together the vinegar and mustard until smooth. Add a pinch each of salt and pepper. Slowly add the remaining 3 tablespoons olive oil, whisking continuously to emulsify the dressing.

3. Drizzle the dressing over the cooled quinoa mixture. Stir in the pine nuts and Parmesan cheese and season to taste with additional salt and pepper. Cover and chill completely, 2 to 3 hours. Stir just before serving to fluff the salad and break up any clumps.

PICKLED BEET, ORANGE, AND QUINOA SALAD

Pickled beets are usually found in the grocery aisle with the pickled asparagus and okra. For this recipe, we used Phat Beets by Rick's Picks. We recommend using a mandolin to thinly slice the fennel bulb. Substitute white quinoa for the tri-colored quinoa if you prefer. SERVES 6 TO 8

⅔ cup tri-colored quinoa, rinsed

1⅓ cups water

2 medium oranges, segmented, juice reserved (see page 67)

2 tablespoons pickled beet juice

2 teaspoons Dijon mustard

2 teaspoons honey

2 tablespoons extra-virgin olive oil

1 cup thinly sliced fennel bulb

1 cup cubed pickled beets

1 cup crumbled feta cheese (about 6 ounces)

kosher salt and black pepper

1. In a medium saucepan over high heat, bring the quinoa and water to a boil. Reduce the heat to low, cover, and cook until the water is absorbed and the quinoa is tender, 10 to 12 minutes. Turn off the heat and let the quinoa sit for 5 minutes. Fluff with a fork and allow to cool.

2. Place the orange segments in a medium bowl and 2 tablespoons of the reserved orange juice in a small bowl (discard or reserve the remaining orange juice for another use). Whisk the beet juice, mustard, and honey into the orange juice. Slowly add the olive oil while continually whisking to emulsify the dressing. Season with a pinch of kosher salt.

3. Add the cooked quinoa, fennel, beets, and feta to the orange segments and toss to combine. Add the dressing and stir to coat. Adjust the seasoning with salt and pepper as needed. Serve cold or at room temperature.

TURKEY "WALDORF" SALAD

This rendition of the classic Waldorf salad, originally made at New York's famed Waldorf Astoria Hotel, is one solution to the conundrum of what to make with leftover turkey. **SERVES 6 TO 8**

⅔ cup white quinoa, rinsed

1⅓ cups water

2 crisp apples, such as Braeburn, cored and chopped

2 tablespoons fresh lemon juice

1 cup cubed turkey breast

2 ribs celery, thinly sliced

1 cup halved seedless grapes

⅓ cup chopped almonds

⅓ cup dried cranberries

⅔ cup mayonnaise

⅓ cup plain yogurt

1 tablespoon honey

1½ teaspoons cider vinegar

kosher salt and black pepper

1. In a medium saucepan over high heat, bring the quinoa and water to a boil. Reduce the heat to low, cover, and cook until the water has been absorbed and the quinoa is tender, 10 to 12 minutes. Turn off the heat and let the quinoa sit for 5 minutes. Fluff with a fork and allow to cool.

2. In a large bowl, toss the apples with the lemon juice. Add the cooked quinoa, turkey, celery, grapes, almonds, and dried cranberries; stir to combine. Keep cool in the refrigerator.

3. In a medium bowl, whisk together the mayonnaise, yogurt, honey, and vinegar. Season with a pinch each of salt and pepper.

4. Add the dressing to the reserved salad and stir to combine. Adjust the seasoning with salt and pepper as needed. Cover the bowl with plastic wrap and refrigerate for at least 1 hour for the flavors to marry. Serve cold.

CHAPTER 5

Soups and Stews

Soups and stews are guaranteed to warm and comfort you on cool nights in fall and winter, but soup paired with salad is also good as a light summer meal. This selection of recipes will satisfy your cravings year-round.

WINTER

Beef Stew

Mulligatawny Soup

Tomatillo and Green Chile Posole

SPRING

Two-Bean Quinoa Chili

Lemony Chicken Noodle Soup

Moroccan Lamb Stew

SUMMER

Bloody Mary Gazpacho

Hot 'n' Sour Soup

FALL

Hearty Fall Vegetable Stew

Aduki Bean, Sausage, and Quinoa Stew

Mushroom Soup

Yellow Beet and Apple Soup

BEEF STEW

Since this stew is made in a slow cooker, it's a good dinner option on a busy day. Simply put the stew on in the morning, go about your day, and finish it within an hour of serving. The vegetables maintain their bright flavors and crispness by being adding toward the end of the cooking process. SERVES 6

2 cups beef stock or broth, divided, or as needed

3-pound beef chuck roast

2 tablespoons canola oil

2 cups dark beer, preferably stout

1 tablespoon Worcestershire sauce

1 bay leaf

1 tablespoon extra-virgin olive oil

2 medium yellow onions, chopped

4 medium cloves garlic, minced

2 medium carrots, peeled and chopped

1 pound sliced white mushrooms (about 3 cups)

1 (15-ounce) can diced tomatoes, drained

1 cup white quinoa, rinsed

¼ cup chopped flat-leaf parsley

kosher salt and freshly ground pepper

1. Pour 1 cup of the beef stock or broth into the pot of a 5- to 7-quart slow cooker and turn the heat to medium.

2. Generously season the beef with salt and pepper. Heat the canola oil in a large heavy pot, such as a Dutch oven, over high heat. Add the beef and sear until the bottom side has browned, 4 to 5 minutes; repeat to brown on each side. Remove from the heat and transfer the beef to the slow cooker.

3. Add the remaining 1 cup beef stock or broth, the beer, and the Worcestershire sauce to the pot in which you browned the beef. Loosen any bits from the bottom with a wooden spoon. Bring the liquid to a boil, then add it along with the bay leaf to the slow cooker. The liquid should cover the beef; add more stock or broth as needed. Cover and cook for 6 hours. Remove the beef from the slow cooker and let cool enough so you can handle it. Shred the beef and return it to the slow cooker.

4. Heat the olive oil in a large nonstick sauté pan or skillet over medium-high heat. Add the onions and sauté, stirring occasionally, until translucent, 5 to 7 minutes. Add the garlic and sauté, stirring constantly, 30 seconds. Add the carrots and cook, stirring occasionally, until tender, about 4 minutes. Add the mushrooms and sauté, stirring occasionally, until browned, 6 to 8 minutes. Add the vegetable mixture, diced tomatoes, and quinoa to the slow cooker. Cook until the quinoa has cooked completely, about 30 minutes longer. Adjust the seasoning with additional salt and pepper as needed. Serve hot, garnishing each bowl with parsley.

MULLIGATAWNY SOUP

Mulligatawny translates as "pepper water" from its original Tamil language of southern India. This rich and flavorful curry-spiced soup is tasty at any time of the year, but it's especially gratifying on a chilly winter night. **SERVES 6**

½ cup white quinoa, rinsed

3 cups chicken stock or broth, divided

1 large apple (such as Red Delicious)

1 tablespoon fresh lemon juice, divided

2 tablespoons extra-virgin olive oil

1 medium yellow onion, chopped

2 teaspoons minced fresh ginger

2 medium cloves garlic, minced

2 medium carrots, peeled and diced

1 rib celery, sliced

1 small red bell pepper, diced

3 tablespoons curry powder

1 tablespoon quinoa flour

2 boneless, skinless chicken breasts, cubed

2 cups coconut milk

½ cup raisins

½ cup toasted sliced almonds

kosher salt and black pepper

1. In a small saucepan over high heat, bring the quinoa and 1 cup of the chicken stock or broth to a boil. Reduce the heat to low, cover, and cook until the stock or broth has been absorbed and the quinoa is tender, 10 to 12 minutes. Turn off the heat and let the quinoa sit for 5 minutes. Fluff with a fork, cover again, and leave on the burner to keep warm.

2. Cut the apple in half and remove the stem and core. Peel one of the halves and grate the flesh on a box grater. Toss with half the lemon juice in a small bowl. Dice the remaining half of the apple and toss in a separate small bowl with the remaining lemon juice. Reserve separately.

3. In a large heavy pot, such as a Dutch oven, heat the olive oil over medium heat. Add the onions and sauté, stirring occasionally, until translucent, 5 to 7 minutes. Add the ginger and garlic, and sauté, stirring constantly, 30 seconds. Add the carrots, celery, bell pepper, curry powder, and a pinch each of salt and pepper, and stir to combine. Cook, stirring occasionally, until the vegetables are tender, about 4 minutes.

4. Stir in the quinoa flour and cook 1 minute longer. Stir in the grated apple and chicken. Add the remaining 2 cups chicken stock or broth and the coconut milk, bring to a simmer, reduce the heat to low, and cook, stirring occasionally, until the chicken has cooked through, about 30 to 35 minutes.

5. Stir in the cooked quinoa, the diced apple, and the raisins and cook 5 minutes longer. Adjust the seasoning with additional salt and pepper as needed. Serve hot, garnishing each serving with sliced almonds.

TOMATILLO AND GREEN CHILE POSOLE

When I was growing up, my mother prepared posole every Christmas Eve—a tradition in her native Santa Fe, New Mexico. My brother and I never ate it, thinking it too spicy, so it wasn't until I became an adult that I appreciated the complex flavors of this dish. This variation on traditional posole is inspired by a version my friend Elizabeth once made with tomatillos and canned green chiles rather than pork, giving it a fresh tartness that nicely complements the mellowness of the hominy. Vegetarians can, of course, use vegetable stock instead of chicken stock.—JH   **SERVES 6**

6 tomatillos, quartered

2 canned green chiles, roughly chopped

1 lime, divided

pinch of kosher salt

2 teaspoons canola oil

1 medium yellow onion, chopped

2 medium cloves garlic, minced

4 cups chicken stock or broth

4 (15-ounce) cans hominy, drained

1 cup white quinoa, rinsed

1 teaspoon ground cumin

¼ teaspoon chipotle powder or chipotle seasoning

diced avocado, chopped fresh cilantro, and red chile sauce, for toppings (optional)

1. Place the tomatillos and chiles in the jar of a blender. Blend until puréed. Juice half of the lime and add the juice to the blender. Add the salt and pulse to combine. Reserve.

2. In a large heavy pot, such as a Dutch oven, heat the oil over medium heat. Add the onion and sauté, stirring occasionally, until softened and translucent, 5 to 7 minutes. Add the garlic and sauté, stirring constantly, 30 seconds. Add the chicken stock or broth, hominy, quinoa, cumin, chipotle, and puréed tomatillo mixture. Bring to a simmer, then reduce the heat to low, cover, and simmer 10 to 12 minutes, until the quinoa is tender.

3. Ladle ½ cup of the stew into the blender (there's no need to wash the blender first). Pulse to purée the mixture into a thick liquid. Pour the blended liquid back into the stew and stir to combine and thicken. Simmer, uncovered, until the stew is hot and the broth is slightly thickened, 10 to 20 minutes. Cut the remaining lime half into wedges and serve alongside the bowls of hot posole along with avocado, cilantro, and chile sauce as toppings, if desired.

TWO-BEAN QUINOA CHILI

In my community, friends and neighbors really rally when someone has a baby—the family with the new addition is treated to a parade of hot meals and baked goods. I often end up making some variation of chili as my contribution; it's nourishing, keeps well in the fridge or freezer, and has healthy ingredients for the new mom. I took this version to my sister-in-law when my nephew was born, thinking the protein in the quinoa and the turkey, and the iron in the beans, would help her recover.—JH **SERVES 6**

½ cup black quinoa, rinsed

1 cup water

1 tablespoon canola oil

1 medium yellow onion, diced

1 medium clove garlic, minced

¾ pound ground turkey or chicken

1 (28-ounce) can crushed tomatoes (preferably fire-roasted)

1 (15-ounce) can kidney beans, rinsed and drained

1 (15-ounce) can black beans, rinsed and drained

1 tablespoon ground cumin

2 teaspoons chili powder, or to taste

1 teaspoon kosher salt

2 teaspoons dried Mexican oregano

Chili "fixings" as desired: shredded cheese, sliced green onions, chopped fresh cilantro, lime wedges, sliced black olives, sour cream

1. In a small saucepan over high heat, bring the quinoa and water to a boil, then reduce the heat to low, cover, and cook until the water has been absorbed and the quinoa is tender, 18 to 20 minutes. Turn off the heat and let the quinoa sit for 5 minutes. Fluff with a fork, cover, and leave on the burner to keep warm.

2. In a large heavy pot, such as a Dutch oven, heat the canola oil over medium heat. Add the onion and sauté, stirring occasionally, until translucent and beginning to brown, 7 to 9 minutes. Add the garlic and sauté, stirring constantly, for 30 seconds. Add the turkey or chicken and cook, stirring frequently and breaking up the meat into small chunks, until the meat is cooked through, about 5 minutes.

3. Add the tomatoes and their juices, kidney beans, black beans, cumin, chili powder, salt, and oregano. Bring to a simmer over high heat, then reduce heat to medium-low and simmer, uncovered, for about 10 minutes to allow the flavors to meld. Stir in the cooked quinoa and simmer until the quinoa is heated through, about 5 minutes longer. Serve hot in bowls, letting each person garnish their chili with the fixings of their choice.

LEMONY CHICKEN NOODLE SOUP

Whenever I felt under the weather as a child, my mom would serve up a bowl of chicken noodle soup along with a steaming cup of lemon-honey water. This recipe combines these two comforting "cures" into one satisfying meal. If you want to intensify the lemon flavor, double the amount of grated lemon zest and lemon juice. Fresh spinach leaves or chopped kale would make for a nice variation.—KS **SERVES 6**

4 ounces quinoa pasta, such as rotelle

2 tablespoons extra-virgin olive oil, divided

2 cups cubed boneless, skinless chicken breast

4 cups chicken stock or broth

1 large leek, finely sliced

1 medium clove garlic, minced

1 medium carrot, peeled and diced

2 ribs celery, sliced

1 teaspoon dried tarragon

½ teaspoon grated lemon zest

1 bay leaf

1 tablespoon fresh lemon juice

kosher salt and black pepper

1. Cook the quinoa pasta according to the package directions. Drain the pasta, return it to the pot, and toss with 1 tablespoon of the olive oil. Reserve and cover to keep warm.

2. In a medium saucepan over medium-high heat, add the chicken breast and the chicken stock or broth. Bring to a boil, reduce the heat to medium-low, and simmer until the chicken breast reaches an internal temperature of 165°F, 30 to 35 minutes. Turn off the heat and strain the chicken, returning the stock or broth to the pot. When the chicken is cool enough to handle, shred the chicken breasts. Reserve the chicken, covered, in the refrigerator. Cover the stock or broth and leave on the burner to keep warm.

3. In a large heavy pot, such as a Dutch oven, heat the remaining 1 tablespoon olive oil over medium heat. Add the leek and sauté, stirring occasionally, until translucent, about 5 minutes. Add the garlic and sauté, stirring constantly, for 30 seconds. Stir in the carrot, celery, and tarragon. Cook, stirring occasionally, until the vegetables are tender, about 4 minutes. Add the chicken stock or broth, lemon zest, bay leaf, and a pinch each of salt and pepper. Bring to a boil, then reduce the heat to low and simmer uncovered, 20 to 25 minutes.

4. Add the shredded chicken, cooked quinoa noodles, and lemon juice, and cook until the chicken has heated through, 3 to 5 minutes longer. Adjust the seasoning with additional salt and pepper as needed. Serve hot.

MOROCCAN LAMB STEW

Preserved lemons can be found in many specialty food stores but are easy to make at home. Wash 4 or 5 lemons and slice into quarters without cutting completely through. Add a layer of kosher salt to the bottom of a sterile canning jar and heavily salt the inside of each lemon. Place the lemons in the jar and press down on them with the back of a spoon to release their juices. Let stand, covered, for 12 to 24 hours. Then add fresh lemon juice to cover the lemons and fill the jar. Refrigerate for at least a month before using the rind. Store in the refrigerator for up to six months. You can also substitute 2 teaspoons lemon zest for the preserved lemon rind in this recipe. **SERVES 6**

¼ cup quinoa flour

½ teaspoon ground allspice

¼ teaspoon ground cumin

1 teaspoon ground turmeric

1 pound lamb shoulder, cut into 1-inch cubes

1 tablespoon extra-virgin olive oil

1 medium yellow onion, diced

1 teaspoon minced fresh ginger

2 medium cloves garlic, minced

1 cup mixed Greek olives in seasoned oil (spicy, if desired), pitted and halved

1 tablespoon minced preserved lemon rind

4 cups beef stock or broth

1 (15-ounce) can chickpeas, drained and rinsed

1 (15-ounce) can diced tomatoes, drained

½ cup white quinoa, rinsed

¼ cup chopped flat-leaf parsley

kosher salt and black pepper

1. In a small bowl, stir together the quinoa flour, allspice, cumin, turmeric, and a pinch each of salt and pepper. Add the lamb and toss to coat the cubes completely with the flour mixture.

2. In a large heavy pot, such as a Dutch oven, heat the olive oil over high heat. Add the lamb and cook, stirring occasionally, until seared on all sides, 5 to 7 minutes. Remove the lamb from the pot and reserve.

3. Reduce the heat to medium. Add the onion to the pot and sauté, stirring occasionally, until translucent, 5 to 7 minutes. Add the ginger and garlic and sauté, stirring constantly, for 30 seconds. Add the olives, 1 tablespoon of the olive marinade, and the preserved lemon rind, and stir to combine. Return the lamb to the pot. Add the beef stock or broth and bring to a boil, then reduce the heat to medium-low, cover, and simmer until the lamb is cooked through and fork tender, 30 to 35 minutes. Stir in the chickpeas, tomatoes, and quinoa. Cover and cook until the quinoa has cooked completely, 15 to 20 minutes more. Adjust the seasoning with additional salt and pepper as needed. To serve, garnish with parsley.

BLOODY MARY GAZPACHO

Since it's served cold, this soup is a refreshing choice for a hot summer day. For a particularly festive flair, float vodka over the top of each serving and garnish with a lemon wedge, a rib of celery, and 1 or 2 cooked peel-and-eat shrimp. SERVES 4

⅔ cup white quinoa, rinsed

1⅓ cups water

3 cups tomato juice, divided

1 medium red onion, diced and divided

1 medium red bell pepper, diced and divided

3 medium tomatoes (such as beefsteak), diced and divided

1 medium cucumber, peeled, seeded, and diced (about 1 cup)

1 tablespoon fresh lemon juice

1 teaspoon celery seed

4 teaspoons Worcestershire sauce

2 small cucumbers, seeded and diced but not peeled (about 2 cups)

kosher salt and black pepper

1. In a small saucepan over high heat, bring the quinoa and water to a boil. Reduce the heat to low, cover, and cook until the water has been absorbed and the quinoa is tender, 10 to 12 minutes. Turn off the heat and let the quinoa sit for 5 minutes. Fluff with a fork and refrigerate to cool completely.

2. Place 1 cup of the cooked quinoa and 2 cups of the tomato juice in the jar of a blender. Purée until smooth, 2 minutes. Add ¼ cup onion, ¼ cup bell pepper, 1 cup diced tomato, unpeeled cucumber, lemon juice, celery seed, Worcestershire sauce, and the remaining 1 cup tomato juice. Purée until smooth, 2 to 3 minutes.

3. Transfer the purée to a medium bowl. Add the remaining quinoa, onion, bell pepper, and tomato and also the unpeeled cucumber. Stir to combine. Season to taste with salt and pepper. Serve cold.

HOT 'N' SOUR SOUP

While this soup is served warm, because it's broth-based it makes a light lunch or dinner option in the heat of summer. To make it vegetarian, omit the shrimp and fish sauce, and substitute vegetable stock or broth for the chicken stock or broth. **SERVES 6**

⅔ cup black quinoa, rinsed

1⅓ cups water

1 stalk lemon grass

1 tablespoon canola oil

3 shallots, minced

2 teaspoons minced fresh ginger

3½ ounces fresh shiitake mushrooms, sliced

½ cup canned bamboo shoots, drained

4 cups chicken stock or broth

1 tablespoon hot sauce, such as Sriracha (optional)

2 teaspoons fish sauce

2 teaspoons soy sauce

2 teaspoons unseasoned rice vinegar

1 cup drained and cubed extra-firm tofu

1 cup medium shrimp, peeled and deveined (41 to 50 ct)

2 cups chopped baby bok choy

¼ cup chopped fresh cilantro

¼ cup finely sliced green onion

1. In a small saucepan over high heat, bring the quinoa and water to a boil. Reduce the heat to low, cover, and cook until the water has been absorbed and the quinoa is tender, 18 to 20 minutes. Turn off the heat and let the quinoa sit for 5 minutes. Fluff with a fork, cover again, and leave on the burner to keep warm.

2. Peel the outer layers of the lemon grass until you reach the tender inner stalk. Cut off the bottom root and thinly slice about 1½ inches of the stalk, starting at the bottom.

3. In a large heavy pot, such as a Dutch oven, heat the oil over medium heat. Add the shallots and sauté, stirring occasionally, until translucent, 5 minutes. Add the ginger and lemon grass and sauté until fragrant, 1 to 2 minutes. Add the mushrooms and sauté until they begin to soften, 1 to 2 minutes. Add the bamboo shoots, chicken stock or broth, hot sauce, if using, fish sauce, soy sauce, and rice vinegar. Bring to a boil, then reduce the heat to low, cover, and simmer 20 to 25 minutes to allow the flavors to marry.

4. Add the cooked quinoa, tofu, shrimp, and bok choy. Stir to combine. Cook until the shrimp is cooked through and the bok choy has wilted, 5 to 10 minutes longer. Serve hot, garnishing each bowl with cilantro and green onion.

HEARTY FALL VEGETABLE STEW

Serve this up on an autumn day when the weather is crisp and cool—it will warm your body as well as your soul. We like to make up a batch of cornbread or to serve it with a loaf of multigrain bread, plus a green salad. Vegetarians can use vegetable stock or broth instead of the chicken stock or broth. SERVES 6

1 tablespoon extra-virgin olive oil

1 medium yellow onion, diced

2 ribs celery, sliced into ¼-inch pieces

3 medium carrots, peeled and sliced into ¼-inch half moons

2 large parsnips, peeled and cut into ½-inch cubes

1 sweet potato, peeled and cut into ½-inch cubes

6 cups chicken stock or broth

1 bay leaf

1 cup red quinoa, rinsed

kosher salt and black pepper

1. Heat the olive oil in a large heavy pot, such as a Dutch oven, over medium heat. Add the onion, celery, and carrots; sauté, stirring occasionally, until the onion is translucent and the carrots are tender, about 10 minutes. Add the parsnips, sweet potato, chicken stock or broth, and bay leaf. Bring to a simmer over medium heat, then reduce the heat to low and simmer, uncovered, for 20 minutes.

2. Stir in the quinoa, cover, and continue to simmer until the quinoa is tender, about 10 minutes longer. Ladle 1 cup of the stew into the jar of a blender and purée. Stir the purée into the stew to thicken the broth. Season to taste with salt and pepper. Serve hot.

ADUKI BEAN, SAUSAGE, AND QUINOA STEW

We're big fans of aduki beans (also called adzuki or azuki beans) because, unlike many beans, they don't require presoaking and can be cooked in about an hour and a half. What's more, they have a mellow, subtly sweet flavor—in fact, in Chinese cooking they're used as a dessert filling. This stew is a perfect one-pot meal for a cold night, accompanied by some cornbread or a baguette.   SERVES 8

1 pound dry aduki beans

1 tablespoon extra-virgin olive oil

1 medium yellow onion, chopped

1 large leek, chopped

2 carrots, peeled and chopped into ¼-inch pieces

2 medium cloves garlic, minced

1 tablespoon smoked paprika

6 cups chicken stock or broth

8 ounces sliced smoked sausage

1 cup white or red quinoa, rinsed

4 cups chopped fresh spinach (5 ounces)

kosher salt and black pepper

hot sauce

1. Place the aduki beans in a large heavy pot, such as a Dutch oven, and cover with water by about 2 inches. Bring the water to a boil over high heat, then reduce the heat to medium-low and simmer, covered, until the beans are tender, 75 to 90 minutes. Drain in a colander and set aside.

2. In the same pot used to cook the beans, heat the olive oil over medium-high heat. Add the onion, leek, and carrots and sauté, stirring frequently, until the vegetables are tender, 7 to 10 minutes. Add the garlic and paprika and sauté for 30 seconds, stirring constantly.

3. Return the beans to the pot along with the chicken stock or broth, sausage, and quinoa. Bring to a simmer over medium heat, then reduce the heat to low and simmer, covered, for 10 minutes. Add the spinach and continue to simmer, covered, until the quinoa is tender and the spinach is wilted, about 10 minutes longer. Season to taste with salt, pepper, and hot sauce. Serve hot.

MUSHROOM SOUP

Puréeing quinoa with mushroom stock or broth not only thickens this soup but also imparts a creamy texture and taste, eliminating the need to add cream. Quickly slice the cremini mushrooms by using an egg slicer.   **SERVES 6**

1 head garlic

4 tablespoons extra-virgin olive oil, divided

⅓ cup white quinoa, rinsed

⅔ cup water

1 medium yellow onion, chopped

2 pounds sliced cremini mushrooms, divided (about 6 cups)

1 tablespoon marsala wine

4 cups mushroom stock or broth

3 tablespoons unsalted butter

½ teaspoon dry mustard

1½ teaspoons dried dill

1 teaspoon fresh thyme leaves

1 tablespoon Worcestershire sauce

kosher salt and black pepper

1. Preheat the oven to 400°F. Cut the top off the head of garlic to expose the cloves. Place the garlic on a piece of aluminum foil and fold the sides of the foil partway up and around the garlic. Pour 2 tablespoons of the olive oil over the garlic and close the top of the foil. Place the packet on a baking sheet and bake for about 1 hour. Remove from the oven and let cool. Squeeze out the roasted garlic cloves into a small bowl and smash with the back of a spoon to create a paste.

2. In a small saucepan over high heat, bring the quinoa and water to a boil. Reduce the heat to low, cover, and cook until the water has been absorbed and the quinoa is tender, 10 to 12 minutes. Turn off the heat and let the quinoa sit for 5 minutes. Fluff with a fork, cover again, and leave on the burner to keep warm.

3. In a large heavy pot, such as a Dutch oven, heat the remaining 2 tablespoons olive oil over medium-high heat. Add the onion and sauté, stirring occasionally, until translucent, 5 to 7 minutes. Add 3 cups of the sliced mushrooms and sauté until browned, 6 to 8 minutes. Stir in the roasted garlic paste and the marsala. Add the mushroom stock or broth and bring to a boil, then reduce the heat to medium-low and simmer, uncovered, for 30 minutes. Turn off the heat.

4. Place half of the cooked quinoa and 1 cup of the stock or broth mixture in the jar of a blender. Cover the top of the blender with a clean towel and hold down as you turn on the blender, beginning on the lowest setting. Remove the towel and the plug in the blender lid, allowing air to escape. Increase the speed to purée and blend until smooth, 2 to 3 minutes, adding more of the stock or broth mixture as needed. Repeat this process with the remaining quinoa and stock or broth mixture, then return to the pot. Reserve, cover, and leave on the warm burner.

5. In another large heavy pot, melt the butter over medium heat. Add the remaining 3 cups sliced mushrooms and the dry mustard, dried dill, and fresh thyme; stir to combine. Sauté the mushrooms, stirring occasionally, until golden brown, 4 to 5 minutes. Stir in the Worcestershire sauce and the quinoa and stock or broth mixture. Season to taste with salt and pepper. Adjusting the heat as needed to keep the soup just under the simmering point, cook uncovered, stirring occasionally, for 10 to 15 minutes. Serve hot.

YELLOW BEET AND APPLE SOUP

Ah, fall! This is a warm and rewarding soup to sit down to after a day of pumpkin picking. Substitute olive oil for the butter to make a vegan version of the soup.   SERVES 6

1 bunch yellow beets with greens (about 4 beets)

1⅔ cups water, divided

4 tablespoons extra-virgin olive oil, divided

⅓ cup white quinoa, rinsed

1 teaspoon ground cumin, divided

1 apple, such as Granny Smith, peeled, cored, chopped, and divided

2 tablespoons currants

3 tablespoons unsalted butter, divided

1 medium carrot, peeled and chopped

1 large yellow onion, sliced

½ teaspoon caraway seeds

4 cups vegetable stock or broth

kosher salt and black pepper

1. Preheat the oven to 400°F. Remove the greens from the beets and reserve. Wash and trim the beets, then place in a baking dish and add 1 cup of the water and 2 tablespoons of the olive oil. Cover with aluminum foil and bake until tender when pierced with a fork, about 1 hour. Remove from the oven and allow to cool. Peel and dice the beets when they are cool enough to handle. Reserve.

2. Meanwhile, in a small saucepan over high heat, bring the quinoa and the remaining ⅔ cup water to a boil. Reduce the heat to low, cover, and cook until the water has been absorbed and the quinoa is tender, 10 to 12 minutes. Turn off the heat and let the quinoa sit for 5 minutes. Fluff with a fork. Stir in ½ teaspoon of the cumin. Add 1 cup of the roasted beets, ¼ cup of the chopped apple, and the currants, stirring to combine. Cover and leave on the burner to keep warm.

3. Wash, dry, and chop the beet greens. In a large nonstick sauté pan, melt 2 tablespoons of the butter. Add the beet greens and sauté until wilted, 3 to 4 minutes. Fold the greens into the quinoa mixture. Season to taste with salt and pepper. Cover and leave on the burner to keep warm.

4. Spread the carrots out on a baking sheet and drizzle with 1 tablespoon of the olive oil. Season with a pinch each of salt and pepper. Bake at 400°F for 15 minutes. Reserve.

5. In a large heavy pot, such as a Dutch oven, heat the remaining 1 tablespoon olive oil and 1 tablespoon butter over medium heat. Add the onion and sauté, stirring occasionally, until they begin to caramelize, 8 to 10 minutes. Add the roasted carrots, the remaining chopped apple, the caraway seeds, and the remaining ½ teaspoon cumin; stir to combine. Cook until the vegetables are tender, 3 to 4 minutes longer. Add all but 1 cup of the roasted beets and the vegetable stock or broth, scraping the bottom of the pot with a wooden spoon to loosen any bits. Bring to a boil, reduce the heat to low, and simmer for 30 minutes.

6. Add 2 cups of the soup to the jar of a blender. Cover the lid of the blender with a clean towel and hold it down as you turn on the blender, beginning on the lowest setting. Remove the towel and the plug in the blender top, allowing air to escape. Increase the speed and purée until smooth, 2 to 3 minutes. Repeat this process with the remaining soup. Season to taste with salt and pepper.

7. To serve, divide the quinoa mixture among six bowls and ladle the soup over the top.

CHAPTER 6
Side Dishes and Pilafs

Pilafs are an obvious choice for quinoa, and we feature several in this chapter. In addition, though, we revamp a few of our old favorite sides and create some entirely new surprises that will help round out any meal.

WINTER

Beet Pot Pie

Quinoa Pilaf with Bacon and Broccoli Rabe

Black-Eyed-Pea Quinoa Pilaf

SPRING

Stuffed Artichokes with Garlic-Lemon Aioli

Creamed Spinach

Spinach and Parmesan Pilaf

Pea, Lemon, and Mint Quinoa

SUMMER

Polenta Fries

Stuffed Tomatoes

Asian-Style Edamame and Shiitake Pilaf

Grilled Quinoa Cakes

FALL

Quinoa Polenta

Quinoa Spaetzle with Browned Butter and Sage

Black Quinoa, Sweet Potato, and Orange Pilaf

Wild Mushroom Quinoa Pilaf

BEET POTPIE

The flavors of this side dish are best matched with a hearty main course such as beef. **SERVES 4**

2 large beets

1 cup water

2 tablespoons extra-virgin olive oil

1 recipe Quinoa–Whole Wheat Pie Crust (page 31)

3 tablespoons honey

3 teaspoons Dijon mustard

1 cup chopped toasted walnuts

1 cup crumbled blue cheese (6 ounces)

3 teaspoons grated orange zest

1. Preheat the oven to 400°F. Trim the beets, place in a small baking dish, and add the water and olive oil. Cover with aluminum foil and bake until tender when pierced with a fork, about 1 hour. Remove from the oven and let cool enough to handle. Peel and dice the beets and set aside.

2. Spray four 8-ounce ramekins with cooking spray. Prepare the pie crust according to the recipe directions through Step 2. Divide the dough into 8 equal pieces. Roll out 4 pieces into rounds about ⅛ inch thick and twice the width of the ramekin. Line the bottoms and sides of the ramekins with the dough rounds. Roll the remaining 4 pieces into rounds about ¼ inch thick and the width of the ramekin. Cover in plastic wrap and refrigerate.

3. In a medium bowl, stir together the honey and mustard. Add the cooled beets, walnuts, blue cheese, and orange zest, and stir to combine. Spoon the mixture equally into the ramekins, filling to the top. Cover each ramekin with the remaining pie dough rounds, seal the edges with the tines of a fork, and poke the tops 3 or 4 times to create air vents. Bake at 400°F until the crust is golden brown, 25 to 30 minutes.

QUINOA PILAF WITH BACON AND BROCCOLI RABE

Salty, smoky bacon is a great foil for broccoli rabe, which has a slightly bitter flavor. This pilaf has quickly become one of our favorites, and it's an excellent way to use up a few pieces of leftover bacon from a weekend brunch. The following instructions are for uncooked bacon, but if you have pieces that are already cooked, just use 2 teaspoons of vegetable oil or extra-virgin olive oil instead of bacon fat for cooking the onion. SERVES 4

3 slices bacon, cut crosswise into ½-inch strips

1 small yellow onion, minced

1 cup white quinoa, rinsed

2 cups water

4 cups chopped broccoli rabe (about 6 ounces)

kosher salt and black pepper

1. Place the bacon in a medium saucepan over medium-high heat. Cook, stirring occasionally, until crispy, 4 to 5 minutes. Remove using a slotted spoon and drain on a paper towel–lined plate. Reserve.

2. Reduce the heat to medium and discard all but about 2 teaspoons to 1 tablespoon of the bacon fat. Add the onion and sauté over medium heat, stirring frequently, until translucent, 5 to 7 minutes. Add the quinoa, water, and broccoli rabe and bring to a boil. Reduce the heat to low, cover, and cook until the water has been absorbed and the quinoa is tender, 10 to 12 minutes. Turn off the heat and let the quinoa sit for 5 minutes. Fluff with a fork, sprinkle with the reserved bacon pieces, and season to taste with salt and pepper. Serve hot.

BLACK-EYED-PEA QUINOA PILAF

Often referred to as Hoppin' John, this traditional Southern dish is thought to bring good luck throughout the year to those that eat it on New Year's Day. To make a vegetarian version, eliminate the ham hock and substitute vegetable stock or broth for the chicken stock or broth. SERVES 6

2 tablespoons extra-virgin olive oil

1 large yellow onion, chopped

1 large red bell pepper, diced

2 medium cloves garlic, minced

1 pound dried black-eyed peas, rinsed and picked through

1 smoked ham hock

1 bay leaf

6 cups chicken stock or broth

1 teaspoon hot sauce, such as Tabasco (optional)

1 cup white quinoa, rinsed

¼ cup chopped flat-leaf parsley

½ cup sliced green onion

kosher salt and black pepper

1. In a large heavy pot, such as a Dutch oven, heat the olive oil over medium-high heat. Add the onion and sauté, stirring occasionally, until translucent, 5 to 7 minutes. Add the red bell pepper and cook until tender, 2 to 3 minutes. Add the garlic and sauté, stirring constantly, for 30 seconds. Add the black-eyed peas, ham hock, bay leaf, chicken stock or broth, and hot sauce, if using. Bring to a boil, reduce the heat to medium-low, and simmer, covered, for 1½ hours.

2. Remove the ham hock. Add the quinoa and stir to combine. Cover and cook until the black-eyed peas are tender and the quinoa is completely cooked, about 30 minutes.

3. When the ham hock is cool enough to handle, remove the meat from the bone and shred it. Cover to keep warm while the quinoa cooks. Then add the ham, parsley, and green onion to the pot, stirring to combine. Serve hot or warm.

STUFFED ARTICHOKES WITH GARLIC-LEMON AIOLI

Pancetta is Italian-style, salt-cured bacon and is found in most specialty delis. Bacon can be substituted in this recipe if you wish. If you prefer the top of the quinoa to be crispy, place the artichokes on a baking sheet under the broiler for 1 to 2 minutes before serving. SERVES 4 TO 8

GARLIC-LEMON AIOLI

1 egg yolk

1 medium clove garlic, minced

2 teaspoons fresh lemon juice

½ teaspoon Dijon mustard

½ to ¾ cup extra-virgin olive oil

kosher salt and black pepper

STUFFED ARTICHOKES

4 artichokes

1 lemon, halved

1 tablespoon extra-virgin olive oil

1 cup diced pancetta

6 shallots, diced (about ½ cup)

2 medium cloves garlic, minced

⅔ cup white quinoa, rinsed

1⅓ cups chicken stock or broth

1 cup grated Parmesan cheese (about 3 ounces)

2 tablespoons fresh thyme leaves

¼ cup chopped flat-leaf parsley

kosher salt and black pepper

1. **For the Garlic-Lemon Aioli:** Place the egg yolk, garlic, lemon juice, and Dijon mustard in the bowl of a food processor. Process to combine, about 1 minute. With the processor running, add the olive oil through the feed tube, beginning with 1 to 2 teaspoons and then slowly pouring in a steady stream until the aioli has thickened. Season to taste with salt and pepper. Reserve in the refrigerator.

2. **For the Stuffed Artichokes:** To prepare the artichokes, cut off the stems and 1½ to 2 inches of the tops where the leaves are tight and fold in on themselves. Remove the tough, outermost leaves and cut the thorny tips off the remaining leaves. Rub the exposed cuts with the lemon halves to prevent discoloration.

3. Fill a large pot with water to a depth of about 4 inches. Squeeze the juice from the lemon halves into the water and bring to a boil. Add the artichokes, cover, and gently boil until any remaining outermost leaves easily pull off, 30 to 40 minutes. Meanwhile, set a wire rack on top of a rimmed baking sheet. Remove the artichokes from the pot and place upside down on the wire rack to drain and cool them enough to handle, about 20 minutes. Gently open up the leaves and use a spoon to scoop out the innermost leaves and the choke, the fuzzy filaments at the very center. If you wish to make 8 servings rather than 4, cut each artichoke in half from top to bottom. Reserve, covered, and keep warm in a 170°F oven.

4. Heat the olive oil in a medium saucepan over medium-high heat, then add the pancetta and cook until crisp, 4 to 5 minutes. Remove using a slotted spoon and drain on a paper towel–lined plate. Reserve. Add the shallots to the pan and sauté, stirring occasionally, until translucent, about 5 minutes. Add the garlic and sauté, stirring constantly, for 30 seconds. Add the quinoa and the chicken stock or broth and bring to a boil. Reduce the heat to low, cover, and cook until the liquid has been absorbed and the quinoa is tender, 10 to 12 minutes. Turn off the heat and let the quinoa sit for 5 minutes. Fluff with a fork. Add the pancetta, Parmesan cheese, thyme, and parsley, and stir to combine. Season to taste with salt and pepper.

5. Spoon quinoa into the center of each artichoke to fill; spoon any remaining quinoa between the leaves. Serve the stuffed artichokes with the garlic-lemon aioli on the side.

CREAMED SPINACH

This side dish is a great vehicle for introducing people to quinoa, since it is a classic, comforting dish that's familiar to most. **SERVES 4**

3 tablespoons unsalted butter

½ small yellow onion, diced

½ medium leek, thinly sliced

1 medium clove garlic, minced

½ cup white quinoa, rinsed

1½ cups chicken stock or broth

8 cups fresh spinach leaves (10 ounces)

1 cup shredded Gruyère cheese (about 4 ounces)

½ cup heavy cream

1 teaspoon grated nutmeg

kosher salt and black pepper

1. In a large saucepan, melt the butter over medium heat. Add the onion and leek, and sauté until the onion is translucent, 5 to 7 minutes. Add the garlic and sauté, stirring constantly, for 30 seconds. Add the quinoa and stir to combine. Add the chicken stock or broth and bring to boil, then reduce the heat to medium-low.

2. Add the spinach, cover, and cook until it begins to wilt, about 3 minutes. Remove the cover and stir the spinach into the quinoa. Return to a simmer, cover, and cook until the quinoa is tender and most of the stock or broth has been absorbed, about 15 minutes.

3. Stir in the cheese and cream. Add the nutmeg and salt and pepper to taste, and stir to combine. Cook until thickened, 1 to 2 minutes longer.

SPINACH AND PARMESAN PILAF

This nourishing, comforting pilaf dish is perfect for kids—its mild flavor is reminiscent of macaroni and cheese. It's an excellent side dish to go with roast pork or crispy oven-baked chicken. Use vegetable stock or a vegetarian chicken stock substitute to make this pilaf vegetarian. SERVES 4

2 teaspoons extra-virgin olive oil

1 small yellow onion, minced

1 cup white quinoa, rinsed

1½ cups chicken stock or broth

8 ounces frozen chopped spinach, thawed

4 tablespoons grated Parmesan cheese, divided (about 1 ounce)

kosher salt and black pepper

1. Heat the olive oil in a medium saucepan over medium heat. Add the onion and cook, stirring frequently, until translucent, 5 to 7 minutes. Add the quinoa, chicken stock or broth, and spinach; bring to a boil. Reduce the heat to low, cover, and cook until the water has been absorbed and the quinoa is tender, 10 to 12 minutes. Turn off the heat and let the quinoa sit for 5 minutes.

2. Sprinkle 3 tablespoons of the Parmesan cheese over the quinoa and lightly fluff with a fork, stirring in the cheese. Season to taste with salt and pepper. Transfer to a serving bowl, sprinkle with the remaining 1 tablespoon Parmesan cheese, and serve hot or warm.

PEA, LEMON, AND MINT QUINOA

It's important to serve this dish immediately so the bacon and chickpeas stay crisp. If fresh peas are unavailable, simply use frozen thawed peas instead. Don't blanch them in Step 3, but add them to the quinoa along with the snap peas in Step 5.　**SERVES 6**

⅔ cup quinoa, rinsed

9⅓ cups water, divided

canola oil, as needed for frying

1 (15-ounce) can chickpeas, drained, rinsed, and dried

2 teaspoons kosher salt, plus more as needed

2 cups trimmed snap peas

1 cup shelled peas

3 slices bacon, cut in 1-inch pieces

1 tablespoon unsalted butter

½ medium leek, thinly sliced

1 teaspoon grated lemon zest

3 tablespoons fresh lemon juice

2 teaspoons minced fresh mint

2 tablespoons minced flat-leaf parsley

black pepper

1. In a medium saucepan over high heat, bring the quinoa and 1⅓ cups of the water to a boil. Reduce the heat to low, cover, and cook until the water has been absorbed and the quinoa is tender, 10 to 12 minutes. Turn off the heat and let the quinoa sit for 5 minutes. Fluff with a fork, cover, and leave on the burner to keep warm.

2. Fill a large heavy pot, such as a Dutch oven, with oil to a depth of about 3 inches. Heat the oil to 350°F. Add the chickpeas and fry until crisp, about 2 minutes. Use a slotted spoon to remove the chickpeas, and drain them on a paper towel–lined plate. Season to taste with salt.

3. Fill a large bowl with ice and water. In a large pot, bring the remaining 8 cups of water to a boil over high heat. Add the salt and dissolve. Add the snap peas and return to a boil. Cook until they turn bright green, 1½ to 2 minutes. Use a slotted spoon to remove the snap peas and immerse them in the ice-water bath until cool. Drain and reserve. Repeat with the shelled peas.

4. In a large nonstick sauté pan or skillet over medium heat, cook the bacon until crisp, stirring occasionally, 6 to 8 minutes. Remove using a slotted spoon and drain on a paper towel–lined plate. Reserve. Pour out and discard all but 1 tablespoon of the bacon fat.

5. Add the butter to the bacon fat in the pan, and melt over medium heat. Add the leek and sauté, stirring occasionally, until translucent, about 5 minutes. Add the snap peas and peas; sauté for 2 to 3 minutes. Add the lemon zest, lemon juice, quinoa, mint, and parsley, and stir to combine. Fold in the bacon and chickpeas using a spatula. Adjust the seasoning with pepper and additional salt as needed. Serve immediately.

POLENTA FRIES

If you're seeking an easy, three-ingredient snack or side dish, look no further. Prepared quinoa polenta, sold in a shelf-stable tube, can be sliced into "fries" and baked to produce an addictive snack. We love these dipped into warm marinara sauce. An oil sprayer such as a Misto Olive Oil Sprayer is one of the best ways to evenly coat the polenta pieces. **SERVES 4**

1 (18-ounce) tube quinoa polenta

extra-virgin olive oil, as needed

kosher salt

1. Preheat the oven to 425°F. Line a rimmed baking sheet with aluminum foil or parchment paper and spray or brush lightly with olive oil.

2. Slice the polenta into ¾-inch rounds, then cut each round into strips about ¾ inch wide. Arrange the pieces in a single layer on the prepared baking sheet. Spray or brush the strips with olive oil, then turn them over and spray or brush the other side. Sprinkle generously with salt.

3. Bake until golden and crispy, 20 to 25 minutes, flipping the fries over halfway through cooking. Serve hot.

STUFFED TOMATOES

These individual stuffed tomatoes make a fun and delicious side dish. Serve them alongside a burger or grilled fish or chicken. Or a serving of 2 tomatoes per person would make for a tasty meatless meal, along with a green salad and perhaps some bread. If you end up with extra quinoa stuffing, it can be placed in a small ovenproof baking dish, topped with grated cheese, broiled until the cheese melts, and served alongside the stuffed tomatoes.   **SERVES 4**

½ cup white quinoa, rinsed

1 cup vegetable stock or broth

4 medium globe (slicing) tomatoes

2 teaspoons extra-virgin olive oil

1 small onion, diced

1 red bell pepper, diced

1 tablespoon chopped flat-leaf parsley

⅓ cup shredded cheddar cheese (about 1½ ounces)

kosher salt and black pepper

1. In a small saucepan over high heat, bring the quinoa and stock or broth to a boil. Reduce the heat to low, cover, and cook until the stock or broth has been absorbed and the quinoa is tender, 10 to 12 minutes. Turn off the heat and let the quinoa sit for 5 minutes. Fluff with a fork, cover, and leave on the burner to keep warm.

2. While the quinoa is cooking, slice the tops off the tomatoes and scoop out the cores, seeds, and pulp. Sprinkle the insides lightly with salt and place the tomatoes upside down on a rimmed baking sheet lined with a double layer of paper towels to drain out the excess liquid.

3. Heat the olive oil in a large nonstick sauté pan or skillet over medium heat. Add the onion and red pepper; sauté, stirring occasionally, until softened, about 5 minutes. Remove from the heat and stir in the cooked quinoa and fresh parsley. Season to taste with salt and pepper.

4. Preheat the oven's broiler. Line a rimmed baking sheet with aluminum foil and place each tomato, cut-side up, on the pan. (If the tomatoes roll, slice off a little piece on the bottom to make a flat base.) Stuff each tomato with the quinoa mixture, pressing lightly with a spoon to pack it in. Top with the cheese and place the pan under the broiler until the cheese is melted and bubbly, 2 to 3 minutes. Serve hot.

ASIAN-STYLE EDAMAME AND SHIITAKE PILAF

There's no reason that rice always has to be the go-to grain for Asian-style meals. With its neutral flavor, quinoa is a great complement for Asian entrées, and black quinoa makes for an especially striking contrast against the green edamame in this dish. This pilaf is excellent with miso-glazed salmon, soy-braised tofu, or teriyaki chicken. SERVES 4

1 tablespoon plus 2 teaspoons canola oil, divided

4 ounces shiitake mushrooms, sliced ¼ inch thick

2 green onions, sliced, white and green parts separated

1 cup black quinoa, rinsed

2 cups water

1 teaspoon soy sauce

1 cup frozen edamame, thawed

½ teaspoon toasted sesame oil

½ teaspoon unseasoned rice vinegar

1 tablespoon sesame seeds

1. Heat 1 tablespoon of the canola oil in a medium saucepan over medium heat. Add the mushrooms and sauté, stirring occasionally, until softened and browned, about 5 minutes. Remove from the pan and reserve.

2. Add the remaining 2 teaspoons canola oil to the pan along with the white parts of the green onions. Sauté until softened, 3 to 4 minutes. Add the quinoa, water, soy sauce, and edamame; bring to a boil. Reduce the heat to low, cover, and cook until the water has been absorbed and the quinoa is tender, 18 to 20 minutes. Turn off the heat, stir in the mushrooms, cover, and let sit for 5 minutes.

3. Fluff with a fork and stir in the sesame oil and rice vinegar to combine. To serve, transfer to a serving bowl or individual plates and garnish with sesame seeds and the green parts of the green onions.

GRILLED QUINOA CAKES

These crisp-crusted cakes are a fun side dish, or they can be used as the base for a saucy dish like stew, a hearty meat ragu, chili, or more. Be very gentle with them while they're on the grill as they're very delicate, and be sure to cook them long enough so they develop a crispy exterior. This will help them retain their shape. **SERVES 4 TO 5**

1 cup white quinoa, rinsed

1¾ cups water

½ cup frozen corn kernels

2 tablespoons chopped fresh chives

⅔ cup grated Romano cheese
(2 ounces)

¼ teaspoon kosher salt

⅛ teaspoon black pepper

1 large egg

canola oil, as needed for frying

1. Spray an 8-inch square baking pan with cooking spray and set aside. In a medium saucepan, combine the quinoa and water. Bring to a simmer over medium heat, reduce the heat to low, and simmer, covered, for 10 minutes. Stir in the corn and cook for 2 minutes longer. Remove from the heat and let sit, covered, until the water is absorbed and the quinoa is tender, about 5 minutes.

2. Let the quinoa cool, uncovered, for 5 minutes more, then stir in the chives, Romano cheese, and salt and pepper. In a small bowl, beat the egg lightly with a fork, then stir it into the quinoa mixture. Press the mixture into the prepared baking pan. Refrigerate until completely cool and firm, about 45 minutes.

3. Heat a grill, grill pan, or countertop grill to medium heat. Brush the grill or grill grate with oil. Cut the quinoa cakes into 9 equal pieces by making two evenly spaced cuts across the pan in each direction. Using a spatula, carefully lift the quinoa cakes out of the pan and place them on the grill. Let cook, undisturbed, until the cakes are browned and crispy on the bottom, 6 to 8 minutes. Gently flip each cake over and cook on the second side until browned and crispy, 6 to 8 minutes. Serve hot.

QUINOA POLENTA

Red quinoa gives polenta welcome color and texture, elevating one of our favorite Italian dishes to an even heartier, more comforting treat. We've chosen Asiago cheese to stir in at the end because its nutty taste enhances the flavor of the quinoa. This polenta can be eaten as is, or topped with marinara sauce or a thick, saucy stew. Or spread it onto a baking sheet, let it chill, and use it to make Polenta Fries (page 103). **SERVES 4**

6 cups water

1 cup coarse polenta (not instant)

2 teaspoons extra-virgin olive oil

½ cup red quinoa, rinsed

2 tablespoons unsalted butter

1 cup shredded Asiago cheese (2½ ounces)

kosher salt and black pepper

1. In a large saucepan, bring the water to a boil over high heat. Sprinkle the polenta into the water, along with a generous pinch of salt and the olive oil, which will keep the polenta from sticking to the bottom of the pan. Stir in the quinoa. Reduce the heat to low and simmer, whisking frequently, until the quinoa is tender and the polenta is thick, creamy, and without any grittiness, 30 to 35 minutes.

2. Remove the pan from the heat and stir in the butter and cheese, stirring until the cheese melts. (If the mixture cools too quickly to melt the cheese, return it to the burner over low heat.) Season to taste with salt and pepper. Serve immediately, or spread in an even layer on a parchment-covered rimmed baking sheet and let set until firm, then cut into pieces and grill or fry.

QUINOA SPAETZLE WITH BROWNED BUTTER AND SAGE

If you don't own a spaetzle maker, there's no need to fret—you can make these by holding a colander over the pot of boiling water and pressing the batter through the holes with a spatula. We recommend using oven mitts to hold the colander, as it will get hot from the steam. **SERVES 4 TO 6**

6 tablespoons unsalted butter, divided

2 tablespoons minced fresh sage

½ teaspoon fresh lemon juice

2 cups quinoa flour

1½ teaspoons grated nutmeg

½ teaspoon salt

5 large eggs

½ cup whole milk

8 cups water

¼ cup grated Parmesan cheese

1. In a small saucepan over medium heat, melt 4 tablespoons of the butter. Continue cooking until the butter turns a light brown color and gives off a nutty aroma, 5 to 7 minutes. Remove from the heat and stir in the sage and lemon juice. Cover to keep warm and set aside.

2. In a medium bowl, whisk together the quinoa flour, nutmeg, and salt.

3. In another medium bowl, whisk the eggs until well blended. Add the milk and whisk to combine. Add the quinoa flour mixture and stir to combine.

4. Bring the water to a boil in a large pot over medium-high heat. Using a ½-cup measure, add the batter to the spaetzle maker and extrude it into the boiling water; stir and cook until the batter is cooked through, about 2 minutes. Remove the spaetzle with a slotted spoon and drain in a colander. Repeat with the remaining batter.

5. Melt the remaining 2 tablespoons butter in a large nonstick sauté pan or skillet over medium-high heat. Add the spaetzle and cook until browned, stirring frequently, 5 to 7 minutes. Turn off the heat, add the browned butter, and toss to combine. Sprinkle the Parmesan cheese over the top, and serve hot.

BLACK QUINOA, SWEET POTATO, AND ORANGE PILAF

Serve this healthy pilaf instead of the ubiquitous sweet potato casserole topped with marshmallows this Thanksgiving, and your family will be requesting it year after year. To serve a crowd, double the recipe. SERVES 6

½ cup black quinoa, rinsed

1 cup water

1 large sweet potato, peeled and diced

2 teaspoons extra-virgin olive oil

¼ cup chopped toasted pecans

1 teaspoon minced fresh rosemary

1 teaspoon grated orange zest

3 oranges, segmented, juice reserved (see page 67)

2 tablespoons real maple syrup

kosher salt

1. In a small saucepan over high heat, bring the quinoa and water to a boil. Reduce the heat to low, cover, and cook until the water has been absorbed and the quinoa is tender, 18 to 20 minutes. Turn off the heat and let the quinoa sit for 5 minutes. Fluff with a fork, cover, and leave on the burner to keep warm.

2. Preheat the oven to 400°F. In a medium bowl, toss together the sweet potato, olive oil, and a pinch of kosher salt. Spread out the sweet potato on a rimmed nonstick baking sheet. Bake, stirring occasionally, until browned and fork tender, about 15 minutes. Remove from the oven and transfer to a large bowl.

3. Add the black quinoa, pecans, rosemary, and orange zest to the sweet potatoes, stirring to combine. Add the reserved orange juice and the maple syrup, and toss to coat. Fold in the orange segments and season to taste with kosher salt. Serve warm or at room temperature.

WILD MUSHROOM QUINOA PILAF

While I was writing this cookbook, my husband and I had the great fortune to be taken by our friends Ashley and Ethan Bisagne of Feastworks Catering to a secret location for a day of mushroom hunting—chanterelles in particular. Upon our return, I couldn't wait to get into the kitchen to cook up our treasures, coming up with this recipe among many others. Feel free to substitute morels, porcinis, cremini, or white button mushrooms for the chanterelles.
—KS   SERVES 4 TO 6

⅔ cup white quinoa, rinsed

1⅓ cups water

1 tablespoon unsalted butter

1 tablespoon extra-virgin olive oil

1 large leek, finely sliced

2 medium cloves garlic, minced

2 cups chopped chanterelle mushrooms

1 teaspoon fresh thyme leaves

1½ tablespoons chiffonade fresh sage

¼ cup Amontillado sherry

¼ cup grated Parmesan cheese

1. In a small saucepan over high heat, bring the quinoa and water to a boil. Reduce the heat to low, cover, and cook until the water has been absorbed and the quinoa is tender, 10 to 12 minutes. Turn off the heat and let the quinoa sit for 5 minutes. Fluff with a fork and leave on the burner to keep warm.

2. Heat the butter and olive oil in a large nonstick sauté pan or skillet over medium-high heat. Add the leek and sauté, stirring occasionally, until translucent, about 5 minutes. Add the garlic and sauté, stirring constantly, for 30 seconds. Add the mushrooms and sauté until brown, 6 to 8 minutes. Stir in the thyme, sage, and sherry. Add the quinoa and Parmesan cheese, tossing to combine. Remove from the heat. Serve hot or warm.

CHAPTER 7

Meat and Fish

Entrées are the heart of the plate. Here you'll find quinoa recipes featuring beef, chicken, pork, fish, and other proteins around which to build your meal. For meatless options, check out the vegetarian recipes beginning on page 145.

WINTER

Horseradish and Sour Cream–Crusted Tilapia

Chicken Paprikash over Quinoa Pilaf

Chile Rellenos

Cabbage Rolls

Shrimp with Pimento Cheese "Quits-Cakes"

Quinoa Pasta with White Beans, Winter Greens, and Sausage

SPRING

Crab Cakes

Grilled Lamb Chops over Greek-Style Quinoa Pilaf

Quinoa Paella

Stuffed Trout

Artichoke and Lamb–Stuffed Crepes

SUMMER

Broiled Salmon on Dilled Quinoa Pilaf

Grilled Pizza with Prosciutto, Grilled Peaches, and Arugula

Fish Tacos

Grilled Scallop Kebabs on Coconut Quinoa

Cod with Tomato-Orange Sauce over Spanish-Style Quinoa

FALL

Stuffed Pork Tenderloin

Turkey, Cranberry, and Quinoa Bake

Chicken Potpie with Quinoa Biscuit Crust

Honey-Glazed Duck with Fig and Pistachio Red Quinoa

Savory Turkey-Stuffed Crepes

Hearty Turkey Sausage Ragu

HORSERADISH AND SOUR CREAM—CRUSTED TILAPIA

Tilapia's a good budget-priced fish option, but it doesn't have a lot of flavor. This easy preparation packs a lot of flavor punch with very little effort.   **SERVES 4**

½ cup sour cream

1 ½ teaspoons jarred horseradish

1 tablespoon minced chives

4 tilapia fillets (about 1 pound)

¼ cup quinoa flakes

kosher salt and black pepper

1. Preheat the oven to 375°F. Line a rimmed baking sheet with parchment paper or aluminum foil. In a small bowl, stir together the sour cream, horseradish, chives, and a pinch each of salt and pepper.

2. Season the tilapia fillets on both sides with salt and pepper and place on the prepared baking sheet. Spread the sour cream mixture liberally over the fish and sprinkle each fillet with about 1 tablespoon of quinoa flakes. Bake until the fish is cooked through, about 12 minutes. Serve hot.

TO TEST THE DONENESS OF FISH

Try this trick from Kelley's mother-in-law for checking when fish is done. Poke a metal cake tester into the thickest part of a fish fillet. If it goes into the fish without resistance, that's the first indicator that it's cooked properly. Next, pull it out and press the tester against your cheek or on top of your hand, between your thumb and forefinger. If the tester feels warm, the fish is done.

CHICKEN PAPRIKASH OVER QUINOA PILAF

This stovetop version of chicken paprikash takes much less time than many of the more traditional recipes. For a twist, substitute quinoa noodles for the quinoa pilaf.   SERVES 4

4 half chicken breasts (about 2½ pounds)

1 teaspoon kosher salt

1 teaspoon black pepper

2 tablespoons plus 2 teaspoons paprika

2 tablespoons canola oil

2 tablespoons unsalted butter

2 medium yellow onions, sliced

2 medium cloves garlic, minced

⅔ pound sliced white mushrooms (about 2 cups)

¼ cup marsala wine

1 tablespoon quinoa flour

2½ cups chicken stock or broth

1 cup sour cream (regular or reduced-fat)

1 recipe Quinoa Pilaf (page 28)

2 tablespoons chopped fresh parsley, plus more for garnish

1. Sprinkle the top of the chicken breasts with ⅛ teaspoon each of salt and pepper and ¼ teaspoon paprika, then flip and repeat on the other side.

2. In a large heavy pot, such as a Dutch oven, heat the canola oil over medium-high heat. Place the chicken in the pot, skin-side down, and cook until the underside is brown and crisp, about 5 minutes. Flip and cook until the second side is browned, about 5 minutes. Remove and reserve.

3. Melt the butter over medium-high heat in the same pot in which the chicken was cooked. Add the onions and sauté, stirring occasionally, until translucent, 5 to 7 minutes. Add the garlic and sauté, stirring constantly, for 30 seconds. Add the mushrooms and sauté until brown, 6 to 8 minutes. Pour in the marsala and cook until the pot is nearly dry, about 1 minute. Stir in the remaining 2 tablespoons paprika and the quinoa flour. Slowly add the chicken stock or broth, stirring constantly until combined. Add the chicken, breast-side down, and cook 20 to 25 minutes. Flip the chicken and cook until it has reached an internal temperature of 160°F when checked with a meat thermometer, about 20 minutes longer. Turn off the heat and stir in the sour cream. Adjust the seasoning with more salt and pepper, as needed. Cover and leave on the burner to keep warm.

4. While the chicken is cooking, make the quinoa pilaf with the parsley according to the recipe directions.

5. To serve, divide the quinoa pilaf among four bowls, top each one with a chicken breast, and spoon the sauce over the top. Garnish with parsley and serve hot.

CHILE RELLENOS

This delicious beef and quinoa variation of chile rellenos features a crispy outer crust rather than the eggy version found in many Mexican restaurants. Serve with black beans and a fresh green salad to complete the meal. **SERVES 4**

8 poblano peppers

kernels from 2 ears of fresh corn or 2 cups frozen corn, thawed

3 tablespoons extra-virgin olive oil, divided

⅓ cup white quinoa, rinsed

⅔ cup water

¾ pound lean ground beef

1 medium yellow onion, diced

2 medium cloves garlic, minced

1 teaspoon chili powder

1 teaspoon ground cumin

1 teaspoon ground coriander

½ teaspoon dried oregano

1 teaspoon kosher salt

1 (15-ounce) can tomato sauce

8 ounces crumbled Cotija cheese

1 tablespoon hot sauce, such as Tabasco (optional)

juice of ½ lime

1 green onion, sliced

⅓ cup chopped fresh cilantro

canola oil, as needed for frying

1. Preheat the oven broiler. Spread out the peppers on a rimmed baking sheet and place under the broiler. Char the skin on each side of the peppers, then remove from the broiler, place in a zip-top plastic bag, and seal. Let steam in the bag for 5 minutes, then take out of the bag. When cool enough to handle, gently rub off the charred skins. Cut a vertical opening in each pepper from stem to bottom and carefully remove the seeds.

2. Set the oven temperature at 425°F. Coat the corn kernels with 1 tablespoon of the olive oil. Spread on a rimmed baking sheet and roast in the oven, stirring occasionally, until beginning to brown on the edges, about 20 minutes. Remove from the oven and reserve.

3. In a small saucepan over high heat, bring the quinoa and water to a boil. Reduce the heat to low, cover, and cook until the water has been absorbed and the quinoa is tender, 10 to 12 minutes. Turn off the heat and let the quinoa sit for 5 minutes. Fluff with a fork, cover again, and leave on the burner to keep warm.

4. Heat the remaining 2 tablespoons olive oil in a large nonstick skillet over medium-high heat. Add the ground beef and cook, breaking up with a wooden spoon, until the beef begins to brown, about 5 minutes. Add the onion and cook, stirring occasionally, until translucent, 5 to 7 minutes. Add the garlic and cook, stirring constantly, about 30 seconds. Stir in the chili powder, cumin, coriander, oregano, and salt. Stir in the tomato sauce and cook until the beef is completely cooked through, about 10 minutes longer. Turn off the heat.

BATTER
2 large eggs
¾ cup pale beer
½ cup quinoa flour
½ cup masa harina

5. Set a strainer over a small bowl and strain the tomato sauce from the beef mixture. Pour the sauce back into the skillet, cover, and leave on the burner to keep warm. Transfer the beef mixture into a large bowl and stir in the quinoa, roasted corn, Cotija cheese, hot sauce, if using, lime juice, green onion, and cilantro.

6. Fill each pepper with about ⅓ cup of beef mixture and close the opening with a toothpick. Lay the peppers on a rimmed baking sheet and place in the freezer for 5 minutes.

7. While the peppers chill, fill a large heavy pot, such as a Dutch oven, with canola oil to a depth of about 6 inches. Heat the oil to 350°F. Line a rimmed baking sheet with paper towels.

8. **For the Batter:** Separate the egg whites and yolks into two medium bowls; set aside the whites. Whisk the yolks and slowly add the beer, stirring to combine but not allowing it to foam too much. Sift the quinoa flour and masa harina into the egg yolk mixture and stir to combine. Beat the egg whites with an electric mixer on low speed until they begin to foam, about 1 minute. Increase the speed to medium-high and continue beating until firm peaks form, 1 to 2 minutes longer. Using a rubber spatula, gently fold the egg whites into the batter until just combined.

9. Remove the peppers from the freezer. Dip them in the batter one at a time and place immediately in the hot oil, being careful not to overcrowd the pot. Fry until golden brown on all sides, 2 to 3 minutes total. Remove from the oil and drain on the prepared baking sheet. Repeat with the remaining peppers.

10. To serve, pour ¼ cup tomato sauce onto each of four plates and top each with 2 stuffed peppers.

CABBAGE ROLLS

This dish is such a tradition in my family that my grandmother even had a special pot reserved solely for making cabbage rolls—a treasure that has been passed down through the generations. While our family recipe is a vinegar-based version, I like the flavors imparted by cooking the quinoa-stuffed rolls in tomato sauce. My aunt Carol taught me the trick of freezing the head of cabbage overnight to make it pliable. —KS   **MAKES 8 TO 12 ROLLS**

1 head green cabbage

½ cup white quinoa, rinsed

1 cup water

1 pound ground pork

1 large egg

1 small yellow onion, minced

¼ cup minced flat-leaf parsley

1 teaspoon fresh lemon juice

½ teaspoon kosher salt

¼ teaspoon black pepper

TOMATO SAUCE

2 tablespoons extra-virgin olive oil

1 large yellow onion, sliced

3 medium cloves garlic, minced

1 tablespoon paprika

1 tablespoon Worcestershire sauce

1 (15-ounce) can diced tomatoes

1 (15-ounce) can tomato sauce

kosher salt and black pepper

1. A day ahead, discard outer cabbage leaves that show any damage. Place the cabbage in the freezer for about 24 hours. Remove it to let it thaw completely, about 3 to 4 hours.

2. Carefully cut out the core of the cabbage and discard. Remove the cabbage leaves until you reach those that are too small to stuff. Cut off the raised center vein on the back side of each leaf so it can lie flat.

3. **For the Tomato Sauce:** Heat the olive oil in a large saucepan over medium-high heat. Add the onion and sauté, stirring occasionally, until translucent, 5 to 7 minutes. Add the garlic and sauté, stirring constantly, about 30 seconds. Stir in the paprika. Add the Worcestershire sauce, diced tomatoes with their juices, and the tomato sauce, stirring to combine. Bring to a simmer, reduce the heat to low, and cook 15 to 20 minutes to marry the flavors. Season to taste with salt and pepper.

4. Meanwhile, preheat the oven to 350°F. In a small saucepan over high heat, bring the quinoa and water to a boil. Reduce the heat to low, cover, and cook for 5 minutes. Strain and rinse with cold water.

The Incans believed quinoa had medicinal benefits and used it to treat everything from tuberculosis to urinary tract infections to appendicitis. They even used cooked quinoa as a poultice for painful bruises.

5. In a medium bowl, combine the partially cooked quinoa with the pork, egg, onion, parsley, lemon juice, salt, and pepper. With clean hands, work the ingredients together. Beginning with the largest cabbage leaves, place about ⅓ cup of filling in the center of each leaf. Fold in each side, then fold the base of the leaf over the filling and roll. Repeat with the remaining filling.

6. Spread half of the tomato sauce on the bottom of a large, heavy ovenproof pot, such as a Dutch oven. Arrange the cabbage rolls in the pot, seam-side down, and top with the remaining tomato sauce. (If you will need to make more than one layer of cabbage rolls, use less tomato sauce on the bottom so you have enough to go between the layers.) Cover and bake until the sauce is bubbling and the quinoa-pork filling has cooked through, about 1 hour. Serve hot.

SHRIMP WITH PIMENTO CHEESE "QUITS-CAKES"

This dish is a spin on the classic combination of shrimp 'n' grits. We substitute quinoa for the grits and add pimento cheese—the epitome of Southern cuisine—to bind the "quits-cakes," a play on "grits cakes." **SERVES 4**

SHRIMP

1 pound shrimp (26 to 30 ct)

2 cups water

2 tablespoons unsalted butter

1 small yellow onion, minced

1 medium clove garlic, minced

1 tablespoon Old Bay seasoning

2 tablespoons pimento juice

1 teaspoon Worcestershire sauce

½ teaspoon hot sauce, such as Tabasco (optional)

3 tablespoons tomato paste

chopped flat-leaf parsley, for garnish

kosher salt and black pepper

QUITS-CAKES

1 cup white quinoa, rinsed

2 cups water

2 tablespoons unsalted butter, divided

1 small yellow onion

1 medium clove garlic, minced

1 (4-ounce) jar diced pimento peppers, drained, juice reserved

4 ounces cream cheese, cubed

¼ cup heavy cream

1 cup shredded sharp cheddar cheese (about 4 ounces)

kosher salt and black pepper

1. Peel and devein the shrimp, reserving the shrimp and shells separately. Refrigerate the shrimp until ready to use. Place the shells in the 2 cups water in a small saucepan over medium-high heat, bring to a boil, reduce the heat to low, and simmer for 25 to 30 minutes. Strain the shrimp stock and reserve. Discard the shells.

2. **For the "Quits-Cakes":** In a medium saucepan over high heat, bring the quinoa and water to a boil. Reduce the heat to low, cover, and cook until the water has been absorbed and the quinoa is tender, 10 to 12 minutes. Turn off the heat and let the quinoa sit for 5 minutes. Fluff with a fork, cover again, and leave on the burner to keep warm.

3. Grate the onion using the large holes of a grater. Melt 1 tablespoon of the butter in a large nonstick skillet over medium-high heat. Add the onion and cook, stirring occasionally, until translucent, about 5 minutes. Add the garlic and cook, stirring constantly, about 30 seconds. Add the pimentos and cook, stirring occasionally, until heated through, 3 to 4 minutes. Stir in the cooked quinoa. Reduce the heat to low, add the cream cheese, and cook, stirring occasionally, until the cream cheese has mostly melted, 4 to 5 minutes. Stir in the heavy cream and cheddar cheese and cook, stirring occasionally, until the cheese has melted, 2 to 3 minutes. Season to taste with salt and pepper.

4. Line a rimmed baking sheet with paper towels. Melt the remaining 1 tablespoon butter in a second large

nonstick skillet over medium-high heat. Using a ⅓-cup measure, divide the "quits" into at least 8 cakes. Press into patties, place in the pan without crowding, and cook until the underside is brown, about 4 minutes. Flip and cook until the second side is brown, about 3 minutes longer. Transfer to the prepared baking sheet and repeat with the remaining cakes, adding more butter as needed. Cover and keep warm in a 170°F degree oven until ready to serve.

5. To cook the shrimp, in a large nonstick saucepan over medium-high heat, melt the 2 tablespoons butter. Add the minced onion and cook, stirring occasionally, until translucent, about 5 minutes. Add the garlic and cook, stirring constantly, about 30 seconds. Stir in the Old Bay seasoning. Add the shrimp stock, pimento juice, Worcestershire sauce, and hot sauce, if using; stir to combine, and bring the liquid to a simmer. Add the shrimp and cook until it has turned pink, about 5 minutes. Stir in the tomato paste and cook until the sauce thickens, about 1 minute. Season to taste with salt and pepper.

6. For each serving, place 2 quits-cakes in a shallow bowl, top with shrimp and sauce, and garnish with parsley.

QUINOA PASTA WITH WHITE BEANS, WINTER GREENS, AND SAUSAGE

To add heat to this dish we call for red pepper flakes, but for a milder version, omit them altogether. SERVES 4 TO 6

1 (8-ounce) box quinoa rotelle

2 tablespoons extra-virgin olive oil, divided

1 pound sweet Italian sausage, casings removed

1 medium yellow onion, diced

2 medium cloves garlic, minced

½ teaspoon kosher salt

¼ teaspoon black pepper

½ teaspoon red pepper flakes (optional)

6 cups chopped kale (1½ pounds)

6 cups chopped rainbow chard (1½ pounds)

1 (15-ounce) can cannellini beans, drained and rinsed

1 cup chicken stock or broth

1 cup grated Parmesan cheese (about 3 ounces)

1. Cook the pasta according to the package instructions. Drain, reserving 1 cup of the cooking liquid. Return the pasta to the pot and toss with 1 tablespoon of the olive oil. Cover and leave on the burner with the heat turned off to keep warm.

2. In a large heavy pot, such as a Dutch oven, heat the remaining 1 tablespoon olive oil over medium-high heat. Add the sausage, breaking it up with a wooden spoon, and cook until it begins to brown, 4 to 5 minutes. Add the onion and sauté, stirring occasionally, until translucent, 5 to 7 minutes. Add the garlic and sauté, stirring constantly, for 30 seconds. Season with salt, pepper, and the red pepper flakes, if using, and stir to combine.

3. Add the kale and cook, stirring occasionally, until it begins to wilt, 2 to 3 minutes. When there is enough room in the pot, add the rainbow chard and cook, stirring occasionally, until it begins to wilt, 2 to 3 minutes. Add the cannellini beans and stir to combine. Add the chicken stock or broth, cover, and cook, stirring occasionally, until the greens have wilted completely and the sausage has cooked through, 7 to 10 minutes. Add the cooked pasta and stir to combine. Turn off the heat and stir in the Parmesan cheese. Adjust the seasoning with more salt and pepper, as needed. Serve hot.

CRAB CAKES

Crab cakes are great as an entrée, but by simply forming smaller cakes this recipe can easily serve as a plated appetizer or even as a pass-around hors d'oeuvre. As an entrée, accompany the cakes with salad and asparagus. **SERVES 4 TO 6**

1 cup mayonnaise

1 tablespoon Old Bay seasoning

½ teaspoon dry mustard

1½ teaspoons fresh lemon juice

2 tablespoons minced green onions, green parts only

½ small red bell pepper, minced

¼ cup minced flat-leaf parsley

2 tablespoons chopped capers

1 large egg

1 pound fresh lump crabmeat

2 cups quinoa flakes, or as needed

1 tablespoon canola oil

1 lemon, cut into wedges

kosher salt and black pepper

1. In a medium bowl, stir together the mayonnaise, Old Bay seasoning, and dry mustard. Add the lemon juice, green onions, red bell pepper, parsley, and capers, stirring to combine. Season to taste with salt and pepper.

2. In a large bowl, whisk the egg. Add the crabmeat and quinoa flakes, combining gently and being careful not to break up the crabmeat. Fold in half of the mayonnaise mixture until the crab mixture just holds together; add more quinoa flakes as needed. Cover and refrigerate for 30 minutes so the flavors can marry and the quinoa flakes absorb some of the moisture. Reserve the remaining mayonnaise mixture in the refrigerator.

3. Line a rimmed baking sheet with paper towels. Form the crab mixture into round cakes using a ⅓-cup measure. Heat the canola oil in a large nonstick skillet over medium-high heat. Place the crab cakes in the oil 3 or 4 at a time and cook until the underside is browned, 4 to 5 minutes. Flip and cook until the second side is browned, about 4 minutes longer. Drain on the prepared baking sheet. Repeat with the remaining crab cakes, adding oil as needed.

4. Serve with the remaining mayonnaise mixture and the lemon wedges.

GRILLED LAMB CHOPS OVER GREEK-STYLE QUINOA PILAF

Roasted vegetables pair well with this dish, which is easily varied by substituting bone-in chicken breasts for the lamb. **Serves 4**

¼ cup plus 3 tablespoons extra-virgin olive oil, divided

1 tablespoon Dijon mustard

1 tablespoon fresh lemon juice

1½ teaspoons minced fresh rosemary

1 tablespoon fresh thyme leaves

4 (1-inch-thick) lamb shoulder chops (about 2½ pounds)

¼ cup chopped sun-dried tomatoes

⅔ cup white quinoa, rinsed

1⅓ cups chicken stock or broth

4 cups chopped fresh baby spinach (5 ounces)

1 teaspoon grated lemon zest

2 tablespoons chopped fresh basil

1 cup crumbled feta cheese (about 6 ounces)

kosher salt and black pepper

1. In a medium bowl, whisk together ¼ cup of the olive oil with the Dijon mustard, lemon juice, rosemary, and thyme. Add the lamb chops, coat with the marinade, cover, and refrigerate for at least 2 hours. Remove from the refrigerator 20 to 30 minutes before grilling.

2. In a small bowl, add the remaining 3 tablespoons olive oil to the sun-dried tomatoes. Let sit for at least 30 minutes to rehydrate the tomatoes. Strain, reserving the olive oil and sun-dried tomatoes separately.

3. Meanwhile, in a medium saucepan over high heat, bring the quinoa and chicken stock or broth to a boil. Reduce the heat to low, cover, and cook until the chicken stock or broth has been absorbed and the quinoa is tender, 10 to 12 minutes. Turn off heat and let the quinoa sit for 5 minutes. Fluff with a fork, cover again, and leave on the burner to keep warm.

4. Preheat a grill pan over medium-high heat. Add the lamb and cook until the underside has grill marks, about 5 minutes. Flip and cook until the second side has grill marks and the internal temperature registers 140°F to 145°F on a meat thermometer for medium-rare, 4 to 5 minutes. Remove from the heat, cover and keep warm in a 170°F degree oven until ready to serve.

5. Heat 1 tablespoon of the tomato-infused olive oil in a large nonstick skillet over medium-high heat. Add the sun-dried tomatoes and spinach; sauté, stirring occasionally, until the spinach has wilted, 3 to 5 minutes.

Stir in the cooked quinoa and lemon zest. Remove from the heat and stir in the basil and feta. Season to taste with salt and pepper, and add more of the tomato-infused olive oil as desired.

6. To serve, divide the quinoa mixture among four plates and top each with a lamb chop.

QUINOA PAELLA

This dish originated in Valencia, Spain, and while a paella pan is especially made for cooking it, a large sauté pan or skillet may be used instead.   SERVES 4 TO 6

½ pound shrimp (26 to 30 ct)

3 cups water

1 large pinch saffron

2 tablespoons extra-virgin olive oil

4 chicken thighs (about 1 pound)

½ pound smoked Spanish chorizo, sliced

1 medium yellow onion, diced

1 medium red bell pepper, diced

1 cup white quinoa, rinsed

1 bay leaf

1 cup clam juice

1 (15-ounce) can diced tomatoes

½ pound squid tentacles

½ pound mussels

½ pound clams

vegetable stock, broth, or water, as needed

1 cup fresh or frozen peas

kosher salt and black pepper

¼ cup chopped flat-leaf parsley

1 lemon, cut into wedges

1. Peel and devein the shrimp, reserving the shrimp and shells separately. Refrigerate the shrimp until ready to use. In a small saucepan over medium-high heat, combine the water and the shrimp shells. Bring to a boil, reduce the heat to low, and simmer for 25 to 30 minutes. Strain the shrimp stock, stir in the saffron, and reserve. Discard the shells.

2. Heat the olive oil in a paella pan or large skillet over medium-high heat. Season the chicken with salt and pepper and place in the pan, skin-side down. Cook until the underside is browned, about 5 minutes. Flip and cook until the second side is browned, 4 to 5 minutes longer. Remove and reserve.

3. Add the sliced chorizo to the pan and cook until browned on both sides, 3 to 4 minutes total. Remove and reserve. Add the onion and red bell pepper and cook, stirring occasionally, until the onion is translucent, 5 to 7 minutes. Stir in the quinoa. Add the shrimp stock, bay leaf, clam juice, and tomatoes with their juices, and stir to combine. Return the chicken to the pan, bring to a simmer, and cook until the chicken is cooked through, about 40 minutes.

4. Add the shrimp, squid, mussels, and clams. If the liquid has been completely absorbed, add just enough vegetable stock or broth, or water, to the pan to continue cooking at a simmer until the mussel and clam shells have opened and the shrimp has turned pink, 10 to 12 minutes. Add the peas and cook 5 minutes longer. Remove the bay leaf, discard any mussels and clams that have not opened, and garnish with the parsley. Serve with the lemon wedges.

STUFFED TROUT

Whole trout makes for an impressive presentation, but do watch for small bones. The stuffing would also be a great base for seared scallops. Sautéed green beans are a good accompaniment. **SERVES 4**

½ cup (1 stick) unsalted butter

1 cup white quinoa, rinsed

2 cups vegetable stock or broth

½ cup chopped flat-leaf parsley, divided

¼ cup minced green onion, divided

3 tablespoons chopped capers

2 teaspoons grated lemon zest

1 tablespoon minced fresh sage

4 pan-dressed whole rainbow trout

pinch of ground sage

2 lemons, sliced

kosher salt and black pepper

1. Melt the butter in a small saucepan over medium heat. Cook, stirring occasionally, until the bubbling subsides and the butter browns, 5 to 7 minutes. Remove from the heat, cover, and reserve.

2. In a medium saucepan over high heat, bring the quinoa and vegetable stock or broth to a boil. Reduce the heat to low, cover, and cook until the stock or broth has been absorbed and the quinoa is tender, 10 to 12 minutes. Turn off the heat and let the quinoa sit for 5 minutes. Fluff with a fork. Stir in a third of the browned butter. Add the parsley, green onion, capers, lemon zest, and sage, and stir to combine. Season to taste with salt and pepper. Cover and leave on the burner to keep warm.

3. Preheat the oven to 350°F. Coat a 9 x 13-inch glass baking dish with cooking spray. Line the bottom of the dish with the lemon slices. Season the inside of each trout with a pinch each of salt, pepper, and ground sage. Fill the cavity with the quinoa mixture; reserve any remaining quinoa, keeping it warm.

4. Place the trout on top of the lemon slices, cover with foil, and bake until the fish is cooked through and opaque, 30 to 40 minutes. Remove from the oven, spoon the remaining browned butter over the top, and serve with the reserved quinoa on the side.

ARTICHOKE AND LAMB–STUFFED CREPES

The caramelized onions add a wonderful element to this dish and can be made a day ahead. Should you have limited time, omit them and simply add chopped onions to the pan after removing the bacon, then sauté 5 to 7 minutes before adding the garlic. **SERVES 6**

1 recipe Quinoa Crepes (page 20)

4 tablespoons chopped flat-leaf parsley, divided

2 tablespoons unsalted butter

4 large sweet onions (such as Vidalia or Walla Walla), sliced

2 teaspoons granulated sugar

4 slices bacon, cut into 1-inch strips

1½ pounds ground lamb

2 medium cloves garlic, minced

1⅓ pounds cremini mushrooms, quartered (about 4 cups)

1 (15-ounce) can artichoke hearts in water, drained and quartered

1 tablespoon grated lemon zest

kosher salt and black pepper

1. Make the crepes according to the recipe directions, stirring 1 tablespoon of the parsley into the batter. Reserve and keep warm in a 170°F oven.

2. Melt the 2 tablespoons butter in a large skillet over medium heat. Add the onions and sauté, stirring occasionally, until translucent, about 5 minutes. Reduce the heat to low, add the sugar and a pinch of salt, and cook, stirring frequently, until the onions are caramelized, about 45 minutes. Turn off the heat, cover, and leave on the burner to keep warm.

3. In a large nonstick sauté pan or skillet over medium heat, cook the bacon until crisp, stirring occasionally, 6 to 8 minutes. Drain on a paper towel–lined plate and reserve. Turn the heat to medium-high and add the ground lamb, breaking it up with a wooden spoon. Cook until it begins to brown, 4 to 5 minutes. Add the garlic and sauté, stirring constantly, for 30 seconds. Add the mushrooms and sauté until they brown, 6 to 8 minutes. Stir in the artichoke hearts and season to taste with salt and pepper. Cook, stirring occasionally, until the lamb has cooked through, about 10 minutes longer. Turn off the heat, add the caramelized onions, lemon zest, and 2 tablespoons of parsley, and stir to combine. Cover and leave on the burner to keep warm.

DIJON CREAM SAUCE

2 tablespoons unsalted butter

2 tablespoons quinoa flour

2 tablespoons Dijon mustard

1 cup heavy cream

2 teaspoons grated lemon zest

4. **For the Dijon Cream Sauce:** Melt the butter in a small saucepan over medium heat. Whisk in the quinoa flour, then the Dijon mustard. Slowly add the cream, whisking constantly until combined. Cook over medium heat until thickened, about 5 minutes; do not allow the cream to boil. Turn off the heat and stir in the lemon zest. Cover and leave on the burner to keep warm.

5. To serve, spoon about ¾ cup filling onto the center of each crepe, fold the crepe over the filling, and roll. Spoon the sauce over the crepes and sprinkle the tops with the remaining 1 tablespoon parsley as a garnish.

BROILED SALMON ON DILLED QUINOA PILAF

Rich, buttery salmon is the perfect foil for the bright flavors of lemon and dill. This delicious weeknight dinner can be made in less than 30 minutes, but it's also a nice option to serve to company. SERVES 4

2 teaspoons extra-virgin olive oil

1 small yellow onion, diced

1 cup white quinoa, rinsed

2 cups water

1 teaspoon grated lemon zest

1 tablespoon fresh lemon juice

2 tablespoons minced fresh dill

4 salmon fillets (4 to 6 ounces each)

kosher salt and black pepper

1. Heat the olive oil in a medium saucepan over medium-high heat. Sauté the onion until translucent, about 5 minutes. Add the quinoa and cook, stirring occasionally, until lightly toasted, 3 to 5 minutes. Pour in the water and bring to a boil, then reduce the heat to low, cover, and cook until the water has been absorbed and the quinoa is tender, 10 to 12 minutes. Turn off the heat and let the quinoa sit for 5 minutes. Fluff with a fork and stir in the lemon zest and juice and the dill. Season to taste with salt and pepper.

2. Preheat the oven's broiler and line a rimmed baking sheet with aluminum foil. Season the salmon on both sides with salt and pepper. Place on the prepared baking sheet and broil until cooked through, about 10 minutes. The salmon is done when it is no longer translucent in the middle.

3. To serve, divide the quinoa mixture among four plates. Top each with a salmon fillet.

GRILLED PIZZA WITH PROSCIUTTO, GRILLED PEACHES, AND ARUGULA

This recipe calls for a grill pan, but an outdoor grill can be used instead to cook the pizzas. Varying the recipe is easy—substitute a basic olive oil and herb dressing or fresh tomato sauce for the goat cheese spread, then finish the pizzas with any toppings you choose. **MAKES 6 PIZZAS**

1 recipe Quinoa Pizza Dough (page 29)

6 cups arugula (about 4 ounces)

1 tablespoon fresh lemon juice

4 tablespoons extra-virgin olive oil, divided

2 peaches

24 slices prosciutto (about 12 ounces)

6 tablespoons chopped shelled unsalted pistachios

kosher salt and black pepper

GOAT CHEESE SPREAD

8 ounces goat cheese, softened (about ⅔ cup)

1 tablespoon fresh lemon juice

⅓ cup extra-virgin olive oil

6 tablespoons chiffonade fresh basil

kosher salt and black pepper

1. Make the pizza dough according to the recipe instructions. Once the dough has risen for 1 hour, divide it into 6 equal pieces and form each into a ¼-inch-thick individual pizza disk. Heat a grill pan over medium-high heat. Place one dough disk on the pan at a time and cook until grill marks appear on the underside and the top begins to bubble, 3 to 4 minutes. Flip and cook until grill marks appear on the second side and the dough has cooked through, about 4 minutes. Remove and keep warm in a 170°F degree oven until ready to use. Repeat with the remaining disks of dough.

2. **For the Goat Cheese Spread:** In a small bowl, smash the softened goat cheese with a spatula until smooth. Stir in 1 tablespoon lemon juice, ⅓ cup olive oil, and salt and pepper to taste. Fold in the basil.

3. In a large bowl, toss together the arugula, 1 tablespoon lemon juice, and 3 tablespoons olive oil. Season to taste with salt and pepper.

4. Heat a grill pan over medium to medium-high heat. Cut the peaches in half and remove the pits, then cut into wedges about ½ inch thick. Coat with the remaining 1 tablespoon olive oil and cook on the grill pan until grill marks appear, 2 to 3 minutes. Flip and cook until grill marks appear on the second side, 2 to 3 minutes longer. Remove from the pan and cover to keep warm.

5. Smear goat cheese spread over the top of the each pizza crust. Lay 4 slices of prosciutto across the top, add about 1 cup of arugula, top with peach slices, and garnish with 1 tablespoon chopped pistachios. Serve warm.

FISH TACOS

If you want to lighten up this dish, you can forgo battering and frying the fish. Instead, season it with ground cumin, ground coriander, chili powder, and kosher salt and black pepper, then cook it on a grill. Halibut may be substituted for the cod.   MAKES 8 TACOS

1 recipe Quinoa Tortillas (page 22)

canola oil, as needed for frying

1½ pounds cod fillets, skin removed

1 cup quinoa flour

1 cup shredded green cabbage

½ cup diced tomato

½ cup chopped fresh cilantro

1 lime, cut into 8 wedges

kosher salt and black pepper

SAUCE

½ cup mayonnaise

½ cup sour cream

½ teaspoon ground cumin

½ teaspoon ground coriander

½ teaspoon dried oregano

½ teaspoon chili powder

juice of 1 lime

1 tablespoon dark beer

½ teaspoon hot sauce, such as Tabasco (optional)

1 tablespoon chopped fresh cilantro

kosher salt and black pepper

1. Make 8 tortillas according to the recipe instructions. Wrap in moist paper towels and then aluminum foil to keep them from drying out, then keep warm in a 170°F degree oven until ready to use.

2. **For the Sauce:** In a medium bowl, stir together the mayonnaise and sour cream. Stir in the cumin, coriander, oregano, chili powder, and salt and pepper to taste. Add the lime juice, beer, and hot sauce, if using, stirring to combine. Fold in the cilantro. Cover with plastic wrap and refrigerate.

3. **For the Batter:** In a medium bowl, whisk together the quinoa flour, cumin, coriander, chili powder, and salt. Whisk the egg in a small bowl, then gently whisk in the beer. Add to the dry ingredients and stir to combine.

4. Fill a heavy pot, such as a Dutch oven, with canola oil to a depth of 4 to 6 inches. Heat the oil to 350°F. Line a rimmed baking sheet with paper towels.

5. Place the quinoa flour in a small bowl. Cut the cod into pieces about 1 inch thick, 1 inch wide, and 3½ to 4 inches long. Pat dry with a paper towel and season with a pinch each of salt and pepper. Dredge the cod pieces through the flour, then dip in the batter to coat. Gently add the fish to the hot oil and fry until it turns golden brown on each side, about 5 minutes total. Using a

In the early 1990s, NASA scientists studied quinoa as a potential crop for a life support system in space because of its high protein content and the fact that it can be grown hydroponically.

BATTER

½ cup quinoa flour

½ teaspoon ground cumin

½ teaspoon ground coriander

1 teaspoon chili powder

¼ teaspoon kosher salt

1 large egg, at room temperature

¼ cup dark beer

slotted spoon, remove the cod from the oil and drain on the prepared baking sheet.

6. Spread sauce on each tortilla, add about 2 tablespoons cabbage and 1 tablespoon tomato, top with a piece of cod, and finish with a sprinkle of cilantro. Serve with a lime wedge.

GRILLED SCALLOP KEBABS ON COCONUT QUINOA

If you have one of those fancy outdoor grills with a little gas burner, you can make the quinoa outside while the kebabs are on the grill. Otherwise, prepare it inside on the stove and keep the pot covered so it stays warm until you're ready to serve your meal. The coconut gives the quinoa a creamy, almost grits-like texture. Depending on the size of the sea scallops and the appetites of your diners, you'll probably need three or four per person. They are pricey, but fresh, high-quality scallops from a reputable fishmonger are totally worth the expense. SERVES 4 TO 5

1½ pounds sea scallops (about 12 to 16)

1 red bell pepper, cut into 1½-inch wedges

1 green bell pepper, cut into 1½-inch wedges

1 (14½-ounce) can pineapple chunks, drained

8 ounces cremini mushrooms

¼ cup plus 1 teaspoon ponzu sauce, divided

2 teaspoons sesame oil

1 cup white quinoa, rinsed

1 cup light coconut milk

1 cup water

2 tablespoons chopped fresh cilantro

¼ cup slivered almonds, toasted

vegetable or canola oil, for the grill

kosher salt

1. Soak 8 to 10 wooden skewers (at least 8 inches in length) in water first for at least 20 minutes so they won't burn, or use metal skewers. Heat an outdoor grill or countertop grill pan to medium-high heat. Thread scallops, red and green bell peppers, pineapple chunks, and mushrooms onto the skewers, using a mushroom on each end to hold the other ingredients in place. Place the skewers on a rimmed baking sheet or a platter.

2. In a small bowl, whisk together ¼ cup of the ponzu sauce and the sesame oil. Using a basting brush, brush the mixture generously over the scallops and vegetables, turning the skewers to make sure all sides get coated.

3. In a medium saucepan, bring the quinoa, coconut milk, and water to a simmer over medium heat. Reduce the heat to low and simmer, covered, until the quinoa is tender and creamy, 12 to 14 minutes. Turn off the heat and let sit, covered, until the mixture has thickened, about 5 minutes. Stir in the remaining 1 teaspoon ponzu sauce and salt to taste, then stir in the cilantro and almonds.

4. While the quinoa is cooking, brush the grill lightly with oil. Arrange the kebabs on the grill and cook until the scallops are opaque and the vegetables have grill marks, about 3 minutes on each side. Remove from the grill to a platter.

5. To serve, divide the quinoa among four plates. Remove the scallops and vegetables from the skewers and serve them over the quinoa. Or pass the quinoa in a serving bowl and the skewers on the platter and let guests serve themselves.

COD WITH TOMATO-ORANGE SAUCE OVER SPANISH-STYLE QUINOA

While the flavors of this dish are particularly well suited to cod, nearly any firm, white fish can be substituted. Piquillo peppers can be found at most specialty grocery stores. **SERVES 4**

TOMATO SAUCE
2 tablespoons extra-virgin olive oil
1 medium yellow onion, diced
2 medium cloves garlic, minced
1 teaspoon dried oregano
1 (15-ounce) can diced tomatoes
¼ cup orange juice
1 teaspoon grated orange zest
4 cod fillets (about 6 ounces each)
kosher salt and black pepper

SPANISH-STYLE QUINOA
⅔ cup white quinoa, rinsed
1⅓ cups water
pinch of saffron
¼ cup diced roasted piquillo peppers
⅓ cup chopped green olives
2 tablespoons capers
½ cup toasted sliced almonds, divided
kosher salt and black pepper

1. **For the Sauce:** Heat the olive oil in a large saucepan over medium-high heat. Add the onion and cook, stirring occasionally, until translucent, 5 to 7 minutes. Add the garlic and cook, stirring constantly, about 30 seconds. Stir in the oregano. Add the tomatoes and their juices and the orange juice, stirring to combine. Bring to a simmer, reduce the heat to low, cover, and cook 30 minutes. Turn off the heat and stir in the orange zest. Season to taste with salt and pepper, cover, and leave on the burner to keep warm

2. Preheat the oven to 350°F. Spray a 9 x 13-inch glass baking dish with cooking spray and spread half of the sauce over the bottom of the dish. Season each side of the cod fillets with a pinch each of salt and pepper. Place the cod in the baking dish and spoon the remaining sauce over the top. Cover with aluminum foil and bake until the fish is cooked through, about 25 minutes.

3. **For the Spanish-Style Quinoa:** Meanwhile, in a medium saucepan over high heat, bring the quinoa, water, and saffron to a boil. Reduce the heat to low, cover, and cook until the water has been absorbed and the quinoa is tender, about 15 minutes. Turn off the heat and let the quinoa sit for 5 minutes. Fluff with a fork. Add the piquillo peppers, olives, capers, and ¼ cup of the almonds, stirring to combine. Season to taste with salt and pepper. Cover and leave on the burner to keep warm.

Incans used quinoa to make a fermented beverage
called *chichi*, which they drank to celebrate
the quinoa harvest. Today quinoa is one of the
ingredients beer brewers use to make gluten-free
beer. Dogfish Head uses it in a beer called Pangaea
(www.dogfish.com).

4. To serve, spoon about ½ cup quinoa onto each plate
and top with one cod fillet. Spoon tomato sauce over
the top and garnish with 1 tablespoon of the remaining
almonds.

STUFFED PORK TENDERLOIN

The tomatillo and pumpkin seed filling for this dish will work equally well with boneless chicken breasts. For a tasty appetizer, use the filling to make jalapeño poppers.   SERVES 6

SAUCE

2 cups quartered tomatillos

1 medium yellow onion, chopped

2 tablespoons extra-virgin olive oil

¼ cup vegetable stock or broth

½ cup fresh cilantro

1 avocado, peeled and pitted

kosher salt and black pepper

STUFFING

⅓ cup white quinoa, rinsed

⅔ cup water

1 cup pumpkin seeds, toasted

½ small yellow onion, chopped

½ poblano pepper, chopped

½ teaspoon ground cumin

½ teaspoon dried oregano

¼ cup fresh cilantro

1 pork tenderloin, butterflied

½ teaspoon kosher salt

¼ teaspoon black pepper

2 tablespoons canola oil

1. **For the Sauce:** Preheat the oven to 400°F. Arrange the tomatillos and chopped onion on a rimmed baking sheet and drizzle with the olive oil. Roast until they begin to brown, about 20 minutes, stirring halfway through. Remove from the oven and place in the bowl of a food processor along with the vegetable stock or broth, cilantro, and avocado. Pulse until combined, about 10 pulses, then purée until smooth, about 2 minutes. Season to taste with salt and pepper. Transfer to a small saucepan over medium heat and warm through. Turn off the heat, cover, and leave on the burner to keep warm.

2. **For the Stuffing:** In a small saucepan over high heat, bring the quinoa and water to a boil. Reduce the heat to low, cover, and cook until the water has been absorbed and the quinoa is tender, 10 to 12 minutes. Turn off the heat and let the quinoa sit for 5 minutes. Fluff with a fork.

3. In the bowl of a food processor, combine the quinoa, pumpkin seeds, onion, poblano pepper, cumin, oregano, and ¼ cup cilantro. Pulse until it forms a paste, 20 to 25 pulses.

4. Spread the quinoa stuffing across the tenderloin, leaving a ½-inch border at the edge of the meat. Roll the tenderloin and tie with kitchen twine about 1½ inches from each end and 1 or 2 times in the center so that it holds together. Season the outside with the salt and pepper.

5. Line a rimmed baking sheet with parchment paper or spray with cooking spray. Heat the canola oil in a large skillet over medium-high heat. Place the tenderloin in the skillet and brown on all sides, 2 to 3 minutes per side. Transfer to the prepared baking sheet and bake at 400°F until the internal temperature of the meat reaches 160°F when checked with a meat thermometer, 15 to 18 minutes. Remove from the oven, cover with aluminum foil, and allow to rest for 5 minutes.

6. To serve, slice the pork into ½- to 1-inch-thick medallions. Fan the medallions out over a serving platter or individual plates, then spoon the tomatillo sauce over the top.

TO BUTTERFLY PORK TENDERLOIN

Two methods can be used to butterfly the pork tenderloin for this recipe. The first is to cut it in half from one end to the other without cutting completely through the opposite side—you want the tenderloin to remain in one piece. Open the tenderloin like a book, lay it flat, and cover the meat with plastic wrap and pound it out to a thickness of approximately 1 inch. The second way is to cut the tenderloin about halfway through from end to end, so the knife only goes in as far as about 1 inch above the cutting board. Gently begin to roll the meat out and continue the original cut at about 1 inch thickness until the entire tenderloin lies flat and is about 1 inch thick. Either method works well. It's really a matter of personal preference as to which technique you use.

TURKEY, CRANBERRY, AND QUINOA BAKE

You can use your extra fresh cranberries, cooked turkey, and mashed sweet potatoes for this hearty and unexpected twist on shepherd's pie. We give the instructions for mashing your own sweet potatoes, but if you already have some prepared, just skip Step 1. You'll probably need 3 to 4 cups of mashed sweet potatoes to top your bake. **SERVES 6 TO 8**

3 pounds sweet potatoes, peeled and cut into 2-inch pieces

3 tablespoons unsalted butter

¼ cup half-and-half

1 teaspoon grated fresh ginger

1 cup white quinoa, rinsed

2 cups chicken stock or broth

1 tablespoon canola oil

1 onion, diced

2 ribs celery, sliced crosswise into ¼-inch pieces

2 medium carrots, peeled and cut into ¼-inch half moons

1½ pounds cooked turkey, cut into bite-size pieces

1 cup fresh cranberries

½ cup sour cream (regular or reduced-fat)

1 teaspoon dried thyme or 1 tablespoon fresh thyme leaves

kosher salt and black pepper

1. Place a steamer insert in the bottom of a large pot filled with a few inches of water. Bring the water to a simmer over medium-high heat, then place the sweet potatoes in the steamer basket and steam until they are tender and mash easily when pressed with a fork, 15 to 20 minutes. Transfer to a bowl, mash the potatoes with a wooden spoon or a potato masher, and stir in the butter, half-and-half, ginger, and salt and pepper to taste. Set aside.

2. Meanwhile, preheat the oven to 375°F. Spray a 9 x 13-inch glass baking dish with cooking spray. In a medium saucepan over high heat, bring the quinoa and chicken stock or broth to a boil. Reduce the heat to low, cover, and cook until the liquid has been absorbed and the quinoa is tender, 10 to 12 minutes. Turn off the heat and let the quinoa sit for 5 minutes. Fluff with a fork, cover again, and leave on the burner to keep warm.

3. Heat the canola oil in a large skillet over medium heat. Add the onion, celery, and carrots and sauté, stirring frequently, until the vegetables are tender, 5 to 7 minutes. Remove from the heat and stir in the cooked quinoa, turkey, cranberries, sour cream, and thyme. Season to taste with salt and pepper.

4. Spread the turkey mixture in an even layer in the prepared baking dish. Spoon on dollops of the sweet potato mixture and use a spatula to spread evenly over the top. Bake 30 minutes or until heated through. Serve hot.

CHICKEN POTPIE WITH QUINOA BISCUIT CRUST

Potpie is one of those nourishing, satisfying dishes that warm the body and soul. If you have leftover chicken or turkey, you can use it instead of poaching your own as instructed in Step 1, in which case you'll only need 2 cups of stock or broth. **SERVES 8**

1 tablespoon canola oil

3½ pounds skinless chicken breasts and thighs (bone-in or boneless)

4 cups chicken stock or broth

2 medium yellow onions, quartered

2 bay leaves

2 tablespoons unsalted butter

2 tablespoons quinoa flour

½ cup heavy cream

1 (16-ounce) bag frozen mixed vegetables, thawed

1 (16-ounce) bag frozen pearl onions, thawed

1 recipe Quinoa Buttermilk Biscuits (page 21)

kosher salt and black pepper

1. Heat the canola oil in a large heavy pot, such as a Dutch oven, over medium-high heat. Add the chicken and cook until browned, turning to evenly brown all sides, 4 to 5 minutes total. Add the chicken stock or broth, onions, bay leaves, and a pinch each of salt and pepper. Bring to a boil, then reduce the heat to low and simmer, uncovered, until the chicken reaches an internal temperature of 160°F when measured with a meat thermometer, about 30 minutes.

2. Remove the chicken from the cooking liquid and place it on a cutting board to cool. When cool, remove the meat from the bone if necessary and cut into bite-size pieces. Strain the cooking liquid into a bowl and reserve. Discard the solids.

3. Preheat the oven to 375°F. Spray a 9 x 13-inch glass baking dish with cooking spray. In a large skillet, melt the butter over medium heat. Sprinkle the flour over the butter and whisk until it forms a paste. Gradually whisk in 2 cups of the reserved chicken-cooking liquid, making sure to stir until smooth after each addition. Whisk in the cream and simmer over medium-low heat until the mixture is thick and creamy. Stir in the mixed vegetables, pearl onions, and reserved chicken pieces. Spread the mixture into the prepared dish.

3. Prepare the biscuit dough according to the recipe directions. Pat or roll the dough to about ¾ inch thick. Use a 2-inch biscuit cutter to cut out 8 rounds of dough and arrange them on top of the filling. Bake the potpie until the biscuits are golden and the filling is heated through, 35 to 45 minutes. Serve hot.

HONEY-GLAZED DUCK WITH FIG AND PISTACHIO RED QUINOA

This is one of my favorite recipes in this book, mainly because of the fun evening I had developing it while visiting my dear friend Kevyn in New York City. I prepared it in his kitchen while he and our mutual friend Jennifer looked on, sipping wine. We enjoyed the meal with a bottle of Côtes du Rhône wine and then, with dessert, drank port left over from the recipe. This is one of the most elegant dishes in the book, and while it's by no means difficult to prepare, it's an indulgent recipe that is ideal for a special occasion or a dinner party.—JH   SERVES 4

1 cup ruby port

1 cup quartered dried Black Mission figs

2 teaspoons extra-virgin olive oil

2 shallots, minced

1 cup red quinoa, rinsed

1 cup shelled unsalted pistachios

2 cups chicken stock or broth

4 duck breasts (about 6 ounces each)

2 tablespoons honey

½ teaspoon hot sauce, such as Sriracha (optional)

1 tablespoon fresh thyme leaves

kosher salt and black pepper

1. In a small saucepan, bring the port to a simmer over medium-high heat. Add the figs to the pan, remove from the heat, and let the figs rehydrate while you prepare the rest of the dish.

2. In a medium saucepan, heat the olive oil over medium heat. Add the shallots and sauté until softened, about 5 minutes. Add the quinoa, pistachios, and chicken stock or broth. Strain the figs from the port, reserving the port. Add the figs to the quinoa mixture and bring to a simmer over medium heat. Reduce the heat to low and simmer, covered, until the liquid has been absorbed and the quinoa is tender, 18 to 20 minutes. Turn off the heat and let the quinoa sit for 5 minutes. Fluff with a fork, cover, and leave on the burner to keep warm.

3. Preheat the oven to 350°F. With a sharp knife, score the fat on the duck breasts in a crisscross pattern, making cuts about 1 inch apart. Place the honey in a small bowl and stir in the hot sauce, if using, and 1 teaspoon of the reserved port. Season both sides of the duck with salt and pepper.

4. Heat a large ovenproof skillet over medium-high heat. Add the duck breasts skin-side down and cook undisturbed until the fat is mostly rendered, leaving a crispy crust, about 7 minutes. Use a spoon or a baster to

remove all but 1 to 2 tablespoons of the duck fat. With a spatula or a pair of tongs, turn the breasts over and brush the skin side with the honey mixture.

5. Transfer the pan to the oven and cook 5 to 7 minutes, or to desired level of doneness. For safety, the meat should have an internal temperature of 165°F when checked with a meat thermometer. Let the duck rest for 5 minutes to allow the juices to redistribute, then transfer to a cutting board and thinly slice each breast on the diagonal.

6. To serve, stir the thyme into the quinoa mixture. Divide the quinoa among four plates and fan the slices of duck breast over it. Drizzle with the remaining port-honey sauce if desired. Serve immediately.

SAVORY TURKEY-STUFFED CREPES

While this dish is a great way to use up Thanksgiving turkey, it works equally well with leftover roasted chicken. Serve with sautéed spinach to complete the meal. **SERVES 6**

½ cup white quinoa, rinsed

1 cup chicken stock or broth

1 recipe Quinoa Crepes (page 20)

3 tablespoons minced flat-leaf parsley, divided, plus more for garnish

4 tablespoons unsalted butter

1 medium yellow onion, diced

2 medium cloves garlic, minced

12 ounces sliced white mushrooms (about 3 cups)

2 teaspoons dried tarragon

1 teaspoon dried chervil

1½ tablespoons quinoa flour

⅓ cup dry white wine

1 cup whole milk

1 cup heavy cream

2 teaspoons grated lemon zest

3 cups cubed roasted turkey

kosher salt and black pepper

1. In a small saucepan over high heat, bring the quinoa and chicken stock or broth to a boil. Reduce the heat to low, cover, and cook until the liquid has been absorbed and the quinoa is tender, 10 to 12 minutes. Turn off the heat and let the quinoa sit for 5 minutes. Fluff with a fork, cover, and leave on the burner to keep warm.

2. Meanwhile, prepare the crepes according to the recipe directions, stirring in 1 tablespoon of the parsley into the batter. Reserve and keep warm in a 170°F oven until ready to use.

3. Melt the butter in a large nonstick skillet over medium-high heat. Add the onion and cook, stirring occasionally, until translucent, 5 to 7 minutes. Add the garlic and cook, stirring constantly, about 30 seconds. Add the mushrooms and sauté until brown, 6 to 8 minutes. Add the tarragon, chervil, and salt and pepper to taste, and cook for 1 minute. Stir in the quinoa flour and cook for 2 minutes. Slowly add the white wine, stirring constantly so that the flour does not clump. Cook until the mixture thickens, 1 to 2 minutes. Turn the heat to low and gradually add the milk and cream, stirring constantly until combined. Cook, stirring occasionally, until thickened, about 5 minutes. Do not allow the sauce to boil.

4. Remove the sauce from the heat and stir in the lemon zest. Pour half of the sauce into a small saucepan, cover, and leave on the burner with the heat turned off to keep

warm. Return the skillet with the rest of the sauce to another burner over medium heat. Add the turkey and heat through, 3 to 4 minutes. Fold in the cooked quinoa and the remaining 2 tablespoons parsley.

5. To serve, spoon about ¾ cup filling in the center of each crepe, fold the edges over the filling, and roll. Spoon the reserved sauce over the top and garnish with parsley.

HEARTY TURKEY SAUSAGE RAGU

Sausage is great to cook with because it adds big flavor to just about anything. Here, it makes a robust sauce for sturdy quinoa pasta. We think uncooked sausage is best in this recipe, but you could also use precooked sausage; just dice it in ½-inch pieces and sauté in Step 1 for about 5 minutes to brown and heat through. This makes a great weeknight dinner—just add a salad and some garlic bread. **SERVES 4**

2 teaspoons extra-virgin olive oil

1 medium yellow onion, chopped

1 clove garlic, minced

12 ounces Italian-style turkey sausages, casings removed

1 (28-ounce) can crushed tomatoes with basil

2 tablespoons tomato paste

2 teaspoons dried oregano

8 ounces frozen chopped spinach, thawed

1 (8-ounce) box quinoa pasta, any shape

kosher salt and black pepper

1. In a large heavy pot, such as a Dutch oven, heat the olive oil over medium heat. Add the onion and sauté, stirring occasionally, until translucent, 5 to 7 minutes. Add the garlic and sauté, stirring constantly, for 30 seconds. Add the sausage and cook, stirring frequently and breaking into chunks with a wooden spoon or spatula, until cooked through, 7 to 9 minutes.

2. Add the tomatoes, tomato paste, oregano, spinach, and salt and pepper to taste. Simmer until the flavors have had a chance to meld and the sauce is thick, about 20 minutes.

3. While the sauce is simmering, cook the quinoa pasta according to the package directions. Drain and add to the sauce pot, tossing to combine. Serve hot.

CHAPTER 8

Vegetarian

Incorporating quinoa into vegetarian entrées is a great way to boost protein and other nutrients needed for a balanced meal. Full of hearty flavor and naturally satisfying, these dishes might have die-hard carnivores not even missing the meat.

WINTER

Quinoa Mini "Meat" Loaves

Balsamic Baked Tofu with Asparagus-Caper Quinoa

Dal with Kale Quinoa

SPRING

Quinoa Pasta with Pistachio-Quinoa Pesto

Spinach and Black Olive Calzones

Quinoa Pasta with Peas, Asparagus, and Lemon Cream Sauce

SUMMER

Lentil-Quinoa Cheeseburgers

Red Quinoa Tamales

FALL

Stuffed Acorn Squash

Eggplant Parmesan

Stuffed Portabella Mushrooms

QUINOA MINI "MEAT" LOAVES

A ketchup-glazed crust and a slightly chewy interior imbue these individual-size loaves with all the best qualities of meatloaf. Serve them with mashed potatoes and a side of steamed veggies. **MAKES 6 (½-CUP) LOAVES**

½ cup white quinoa, rinsed

1 cup water

2 teaspoons extra-virgin olive oil

1 small onion, diced

2 small carrots, peeled and diced

8 ounces white mushrooms, quartered

1 medium clove garlic, minced

1 (12-ounce) bag meatless crumbles

1 tablespoon plus ½ teaspoon soy sauce, divided

1 teaspoon dried thyme

1 large egg, lightly beaten

¼ cup plus 2 tablespoons ketchup, divided

⅛ teaspoon kosher salt

pinch of black pepper

1. In a small saucepan over high heat, bring the quinoa and water to a boil. Reduce the heat to low, cover, and cook until the water has been absorbed and the quinoa is tender, 10 to 12 minutes. Turn off the heat and let the quinoa sit for 5 minutes. Fluff with a fork and allow to cool.

2. Preheat the oven to 350°F. Line a rimmed baking sheet with aluminum foil and spray with cooking spray. In a large nonstick skillet, heat the olive oil over medium-high heat. Add the onion and carrots, and sauté until softened, 5 to 7 minutes.

3. While the carrots and onion are cooking, put the mushrooms in a food processor and pulse several times until finely minced. Add the garlic to the skillet with the onion and carrots; sauté, stirring constantly, for 30 seconds. Add the mushrooms and sauté, stirring occasionally, until the mushrooms release their liquid and it evaporates, 7 to 9 minutes. The mushrooms should look mushy and pastelike. Season with the salt and black pepper.

4. Add the meatless crumbles, 1 tablespoon of the soy sauce, and the thyme to the skillet and cook, stirring occasionally, until the crumbles are heated through, 4 to 5 minutes. Transfer the mixture to a large bowl, stir in the cooked quinoa, and let cool for 5 minutes, stirring occasionally.

5. Stir in the egg and ¼ cup of the ketchup. Pack the mixture into a ½ cup measuring cup and turn out onto the prepared baking sheet to make 6 meatloaves. If there is any mixture left, press a little extra into the top of each loaf. In a small bowl, stir together the remaining 2 tablespoons ketchup and ½ teaspoon soy sauce. Brush onto the top of each loaf. Bake until the meatloaves develop a light crust, 40 to 45 minutes. Serve hot.

BALSAMIC BAKED TOFU WITH ASPARAGUS-CAPER QUINOA

If you cook with tofu a lot, it's worth investing in a tofu press, available online or in a kitchenware store. Otherwise, two plates and a couple cans of food can make an adequate, if slightly precarious, substitute. Another handy gadget is an oil sprayer, such as a Misto, to coat the tofu evenly with oil. A pastry or basting brush works if you don't have a sprayer. **SERVES 4**

1 (14-ounce) block extra-firm tofu, drained

¼ cup balsamic vinegar

olive oil spray

¼ teaspoon kosher salt, plus more as needed

2 teaspoons extra-virgin olive oil

3 shallots, chopped

1 cup white quinoa, rinsed

1¾ cups vegetable stock or broth

12 ounces asparagus, cut into 1-inch pieces

2 tablespoons capers

2 tablespoons grated Parmesan cheese, or as needed

black pepper

1. Press the block of tofu in a tofu press or under a weighted plate for 20 to 30 minutes to press out as much water as possible and create a firmer texture.

2. Preheat the oven to 400°F. Line a rimmed baking sheet with parchment paper. Cut the tofu into 1-inch cubes and place in a medium bowl. Drizzle with the balsamic vinegar and carefully toss to coat completely. Remove the tofu from the bowl, reserving the remaining vinegar, and arrange the cubes on the prepared baking sheet. Lightly spray or brush with olive oil and sprinkle with ¼ teaspoon salt. Bake until lightly browned and chewy, about 40 minutes, brushing with more vinegar about halfway through.

3. Meanwhile, heat the olive oil in a medium saucepan over medium heat. Add the shallots and sauté until tender, about 5 minutes. Add the quinoa and sauté, stirring, until the quinoa is lightly browned, 3 to 5 minutes. Pour in the stock or broth and bring to a simmer, then reduce the heat to low, cover, and simmer for 7 minutes. Add the asparagus and capers, then simmer until the liquid has been absorbed and the quinoa is tender, 7 to 10 minutes longer. Remove from the heat, stir in the Parmesan cheese, and season to taste with pepper and more salt as needed.

4. To serve, divide the quinoa among four plates or shallow pasta bowls. Top with the baked tofu and sprinkle with additional Parmesan cheese, if desired.

DAL WITH KALE QUINOA

This dish is a meal on its own, or it can be served as a side dish for most Indian-inspired dinners. To cut the chiffonade, simply stack the kale leaves, roll them into a "cigar," and thinly slice, starting at one end, to form thin ribbons. This technique allows the kale to wilt quickly. SERVES 4 TO 6

1 cup white quinoa, rinsed

2 cups water

2 tablespoons extra-virgin olive oil

2 medium cloves garlic, minced

4 cups chiffonade kale leaves
(about 12 ounces)

1½ tablespoons fresh lemon juice

kosher salt and black pepper

LENTILS

2 tablespoons extra-virgin olive oil

1 medium yellow onion, sliced

2 medium cloves garlic, minced

1 tablespoon minced fresh ginger

1 tablespoon garam masala

1 teaspoon ground turmeric

1 cup French green lentils

4 cups vegetable stock or broth

1 bay leaf

1 (15-ounce) can diced tomatoes

kosher salt and black pepper

1. In a small saucepan over high heat, bring the quinoa and water to a boil. Reduce the heat to low, cover, and cook until the water has been absorbed and the quinoa is tender, 10 to 12 minutes. Turn off the heat and let the quinoa sit for 5 minutes. Fluff with a fork, cover, and leave on the burner to keep warm.

2. **For the Lentils:** Heat the olive oil in a large heavy pot, such as a Dutch oven, over medium-high heat. Add the onion and sauté, stirring occasionally, until translucent, 5 to 7 minutes. Add the garlic and ginger; cook, stirring constantly, about 30 seconds. Stir in the garam masala and turmeric, stir in the lentils, and add the vegetable stock or broth and bay leaf. Bring to a boil, reduce the heat to medium-low, cover, and simmer for 30 minutes. Uncover and add the tomatoes with their juice. Return to a boil over medium-high heat, reduce the heat to medium-low, cover, and simmer until the lentils are tender, 30 to 40 minutes longer. Season to taste with salt and pepper. Turn off the heat and leave on the burner to keep warm.

3. Heat the olive oil in a nonstick sauté pan or skillet over medium heat. Add the garlic and cook, stirring constantly, about 30 seconds. Add the kale, stir to combine, and cook until it begins to wilt, 2 to 3 minutes longer. Add the lemon juice and continue to cook for 1 to 2 minutes more. Stir in the cooked quinoa and season to taste with salt and pepper. Serve the lentils over the quinoa.

QUINOA PASTA WITH PISTACHIO-QUINOA PESTO

Simply adding quinoa and toasted pistachios changes the entire flavor of traditional basil pesto. The pesto freezes well, so make extra for your freezer and thaw it when you need a delicious dish in minutes. It works well as a stuffing or topping for an array of grilled goodies. **SERVES 4 TO 6**

⅓ cup white quinoa, rinsed

⅔ cup water

1 cup toasted shelled unsalted pistachios

½ cup toasted pine nuts

¾ cup grated Parmesan cheese (about 2½ ounces), plus more to serve

¼ cup chopped flat-leaf parsley

1 cup chopped fresh basil

1 cup plus 1 tablespoon extra-virgin olive oil, divided

1 (8-ounce) box quinoa fettuccine

kosher salt and black pepper

1. In a small saucepan over high heat, bring the quinoa and water to a boil. Reduce the heat to low, cover, and cook until the water has been absorbed and the quinoa is tender, 10 to 12 minutes. Turn off the heat and let the quinoa sit for 5 minutes. Fluff with a fork and allow to cool.

2. In the bowl of a food processor, combine the pistachios, pine nuts, Parmesan cheese, and cooked quinoa. Pulse until the nuts are finely chopped, about 15 long pulses. Add the parsley and basil and pulse until combined, about 10 quick pulses. With the food processor running, slowly add 1 cup of the olive oil in a steady stream through the feed tube until well combined. The pesto will be thick. Set aside.

3. Cook the quinoa pasta according to the package directions. Drain, reserving 1 cup of the cooking liquid. Return the pasta to the pot, add the pesto, and toss to coat. If the pesto seems too thick, add the reserved pasta water 1 tablespoon at a time until the desired consistency is reached. Season to taste with salt and a few grinds of pepper. Top with additional Parmesan cheese, if desired. Serve hot or warm.

SPINACH AND BLACK OLIVE CALZONES

My family loves calzone night; the kids can play with extra chunks of dough or even fill their own calzones with toppings of their choosing. I love the spinach and black olive combination, but you can use whatever fillings you like. Some of our other favorites are roasted red peppers, canned artichoke hearts, meat or veggie sausage, and wilted arugula. If you have a favorite homemade pizza sauce recipe, feel free to use it; you'll need about 4 cups.—JH **MAKES 4 CALZONES**

2 recipes Quinoa Pizza Dough (page 29)

cornmeal or semolina flour, for baking sheet

4 cups prepared pizza sauce

2 (10-ounce) packages frozen spinach, thawed and squeezed to remove excess water

1 cup sliced black olives

1 cup shredded mozzarella cheese (about 4 ounces)

1. Prepare the pizza dough according to the recipe instructions, making a double batch.

2. Preheat the oven to 450°F; if you have a pizza stone, put it in the oven before preheating. If you don't have a pizza stone, sprinkle a rimmed nonstick baking sheet lightly with cornmeal or semolina flour. Heat the pizza sauce in a medium saucepan and keep warm over low heat.

3. Divide the dough into four equal pieces. Work with one piece at a time, keeping the other pieces covered with a towel or plastic wrap so they don't dry out. On a work surface lightly dusted with flour, use your hands to pat and stretch a piece of dough into a flat oval about 12 x 8 inches. Arrange a quarter each of the spinach and black olives on half of the oval, leaving an edge of about 1 inch uncovered. Sprinkle with about ¼ cup mozzarella cheese and drizzle with about ¼ cup pizza sauce. Fold the dough over the filling and, beginning at one end, roll the edge to seal. Tuck the rolled edge under the calzone. Carefully transfer the finished calzone to the baking sheet or slide onto the hot pizza stone in the oven.

4. Repeat with the remaining dough and the filling. Bake the calzones until the dough is golden and they sound hollow when tapped, about 15 minutes. Serve hot with the remaining pizza sauce spooned over.

QUINOA PASTA WITH PEAS, ASPARAGUS, AND LEMON CREAM SAUCE

Quinoa pasta cooks beautifully, and the flavor is neutral enough to be compatible with any sauce. This lemon-cream sauce becomes thick and rich with the addition of quinoa and Parmesan cheese. If fresh peas are unavailable, simply use frozen thawed peas instead. Don't blanch them in Step 4— just add them to the quinoa along with the asparagus in Step 6. SERVES 4 TO 6

⅓ cup white quinoa, rinsed

1⅔ cups vegetable stock or broth, divided

8 cups water

2 teaspoons kosher salt, plus more as needed

¾ pound asparagus, cut into 1-inch pieces

1 cup shelled peas

1 (8-ounce) box quinoa rotelle

3 tablespoons unsalted butter, divided

1 cup heavy cream

2 medium cloves garlic, minced

½ cup white wine

2 teaspoons grated lemon zest

3 tablespoons fresh lemon juice

2 tablespoons chopped flat-leaf parsley

1 cup grated Parmesan cheese (about 3 ounces), plus more to serve

black pepper

1. In a small saucepan over high heat, bring the quinoa and ⅔ cup of the vegetable stock or broth to a boil. Reduce the heat to low, cover, and cook until the liquid has been absorbed and the quinoa is tender, 10 to 12 minutes. Turn off the heat and let the quinoa sit for 5 minutes. Fluff with a fork and allow to cool.

2. In a blender, puree the cooked quinoa and the remaining 1 cup vegetable stock or broth until smooth, 1 to 2 minutes. Return to the pot, cover, and leave on the burner to keep warm.

3. Fill a large bowl with ice and water. In a large saucepot, bring the 8 cups water to a boil over high heat. Add 2 teaspoons salt and stir to dissolve. Add the asparagus and submerge with a spoon. Cook until the color turns bright green, 2 to 4 minutes depending on the thickness of the asparagus. Using a slotted spoon, transfer the asparagus to the ice water bath to cool, then drain and set aside.

4. If you are using fresh peas, cook them the same way but for just 45 to 60 seconds before transferring them to an ice water bath.

5. Cook the pasta according to the package instructions. Drain, reserving 1 cup of the cooking liquid. Return the pasta to the pot and toss with 1 tablespoon of the butter. Cover to keep warm.

6. While the pasta is cooking, make the cream sauce. Gently heat the cream in a small saucepan over medium heat. In a large saucepan over medium-high heat, melt 2 tablespoons of the butter, add the garlic and cook, stirring constantly, about 30 seconds. Add the asparagus, peas, and white wine. Cook until the wine has reduced by at least half, 3 to 4 minutes. Stir in the quinoa purée and heat through, about 2 minutes. Turn off the heat and stir in the warm cream, lemon zest, and juice. Leave on the warm burner to thicken, 2 to 3 minutes.

7. Stir in the parsley, then add the pasta and toss to combine. Stir in the Parmesan cheese and let sit until the cheese is melted, about 1 minute. If the sauce is too thick, add the reserved pasta water 1 tablespoon at a time until the desired consistency is reached. Season to taste with salt and pepper. Top with additional Parmesan cheese, if desired.

LENTIL-QUINOA CHEESEBURGERS

These "burgers" have a tender interior but a nice crust on the outside. They're a great veggie option when you're sick of store-bought frozen meatless patties. The smoked paprika adds a nice flavor, so it's worth seeking out at a supermarket or specialty food store that has a well-stocked spice aisle. Extra cooked burgers without cheese freeze well. You can reheat them in the oven or microwave, on the grill, or on the stovetop, just as you'd prepare commercial frozen burgers. **Makes 8 Burgers**

1 cup white quinoa, rinsed

5 cups water, divided

2 teaspoons extra-virgin olive oil

½ small yellow onion, minced

1 medium carrot, diced

1 rib celery, diced

1 cup brown lentils

1 medium red bell pepper, diced

1 tablespoon soy sauce

1 teaspoon smoked paprika

½ teaspoon garlic powder

½ teaspoon kosher salt

black pepper

1 large egg, lightly beaten

½ cup quinoa flakes

canola oil, as needed

6 slices American or cheddar cheese

6 hamburger buns

lettuce leaves, sliced tomatoes, ketchup, mustard, or other condiments

1. In a medium saucepan over high heat, bring the quinoa and 2 cups of the water to a boil. Reduce the heat to low, cover, and cook until the water has been absorbed and the quinoa is tender, 10 to 12 minutes. Turn off the heat and let the quinoa sit for 5 minutes. Fluff with a fork and allow to cool.

2. In a large saucepan, heat the olive oil over medium heat. Add the onion, carrot, and celery, and sauté until tender, about 5 minutes. Add the lentils and the remaining 3 cups water, and simmer until the lentils are tender, about 20 minutes. Strain.

3. In a blender, purée the lentil mixture with the bell pepper until they form a slightly chunky paste. Add the soy sauce, paprika, garlic powder, a generous pinch of salt, and a pinch of black pepper; pulse to combine. Transfer the purée to a bowl and stir in the egg, then stir in the cooked quinoa and quinoa flakes. The mixture should be about as thick as mashed potatoes and able to loosely hold its shape.

4. Using about ½ cup of the mixture for each burger, form into patties. Place on a plate or baking sheet and refrigerate for at least 30 minutes, or as long as several hours, to allow the burgers to firm up.

5. Heat about 2 tablespoons of canola oil in a large nonstick skillet, griddle, or grill pan over medium-high heat. When the oil is hot, place the burgers in the pan, working in batches if necessary to avoid overcrowding.

Cook until the underside is browned and crisp, about 8 minutes, then flip and cook until the second side is browned and crisp, 6 to 8 minutes longer. Top with cheese and either cover the pan or put the burgers under a broiler for 1 minute to melt the cheese. Serve on buns with your choice of condiments.

RED QUINOA TAMALES

I once had red quinoa tamales at a restaurant in Albuquerque and was eager to try making my own version. The cornhusk tamale wrappers can be hard to find, but most Mexican grocery stores and some gourmet shops or natural food stores carry them. If all else fails, you might be able to persuade a local Mexican restaurant to sell you some.—JH **Makes about 1 Dozen Tamales**

13 to 15 dried cornhusks for tamales

1 cup red quinoa, rinsed

2 cups water

2 cups frozen corn kernels, thawed, or fresh corn, steamed until tender

2 teaspoons ground cumin

½ teaspoon kosher salt

1 canned chipotle pepper in adobo, diced

1 tablespoon tomato paste

1 ½ cups shredded Monterey jack cheese (about 4 ounces)

1. Submerge the cornhusks in a deep container of water until they're soft and pliant, about 20 minutes.

2. In a small saucepan over high heat, bring the quinoa and water to a boil. Reduce the heat to low, cover, and cook until the water has been absorbed and the quinoa is tender, 18 to 20 minutes. Turn off the heat and let the quinoa sit for 5 minutes. Fluff with a fork and allow to cool.

3. In a large bowl, combine the quinoa with all the remaining ingredients.

4. Remove the husks from the water and blot them with a towel or paper towels to remove excess moisture. Keep them under a damp towel or in a large zip-top plastic bag as you're working so they don't dry out.

5. Spoon about ¼ cup filling onto the middle of a cornhusk. Fold the long sides of the husk over the filling, then roll the husk over the filling, beginning with one short end and overlapping the husk edges to completely enclose the filling. Tie kitchen twine or a long piece of an extra cornhusk around the tamale to keep it from opening during cooking. Repeat with the remaining wrappers.

6. Place the tamales in a steamer basket over simmering water or a rice cooker with a steamer insert and steam until heated through, about 45 minutes.

STUFFED ACORN SQUASH

A delicious main course whether you're a vegetarian or not, this stuffed squash strikes that perfect balance between sweet and savory. This recipe is a fun option for a dinner party and can be prepared ahead of time—just follow Steps 1 to 4 and refrigerate the squash, wrapped in plastic wrap or aluminum foil, for up to one day, then roast as instructed in Step 5. Allow 30 to 40 minutes for the squash to heat through if it has been stored in the refrigerator. **SERVES 4**

2 acorn squash, halved stem to end, seeds removed

1 tablespoon extra-virgin olive oil

1 tablespoon unsalted butter

½ cup red or white quinoa, rinsed

1 cup water

1 shallot, minced

2½ to 3 cups fresh baby spinach (about 3 ounces)

⅓ cup currants or golden raisins

⅓ cup chopped shelled unsalted pistachios

2 tablespoons plus 4 teaspoons grated Parmesan cheese, divided

kosher salt and black pepper

1. Preheat the oven to 400°F. Line a rimmed baking sheet with parchment paper or aluminum foil. Brush the insides of the squash with olive oil and sprinkle lightly with salt and pepper. Place cut-side down on the prepared baking sheet. Roast until the flesh can be pierced easily with a fork, about 30 minutes.

2. Meanwhile, in a small saucepan over high heat, bring the quinoa and water to a boil. Reduce the heat to low, cover, and cook until the water has been absorbed and the quinoa is tender, 10 to 12 minutes for white quinoa, 18 to 20 minutes for red. Turn off the heat and let the quinoa sit for 5 minutes. Fluff with a fork and allow to cool slightly.

3. In a large nonstick skillet, melt the butter over medium heat. Add the shallot and sauté, stirring occasionally, until translucent and soft, 3 to 5 minutes. Add the spinach and wilt, stirring and turning occasionally with tongs, 3 to 4 minutes. Stir in the cooked quinoa, raisins or currants, pistachios, and 2 tablespoons of Parmesan cheese. Season to taste with salt and pepper.

4. When the squash are cooked, turn them over so the cut side is up. Fill each half completely with filling and sprinkle with about 1 teaspoon of the remaining Parmesan cheese.

5. Return the filled squash to the oven and cook an additional 20 to 25 minutes, until the filling is heated through and the cheese is melted. Serve hot.

EGGPLANT PARMESAN

For the tomato sauce, we recommend using organic tomatoes containing the least amount of salt and other additives. While this dish requires a number of preparation steps, we think you'll find it well worth the effort. SERVES 4 TO 6

TOMATO SAUCE

1 tablespoon extra-virgin olive oil

1 medium yellow onion, diced

2 medium cloves garlic, minced

1 teaspoon dried oregano

½ teaspoon dried thyme

½ teaspoon red pepper flakes (optional)

⅓ cup red wine

1 (28-ounce) can diced tomatoes

kosher salt and black pepper

⅓ cup white quinoa, rinsed

⅔ cup water

1 large eggplant

4 tablespoons kosher salt, or as needed

1½ cups (3 recipes) Quinoa Frying Batter (page 25)

1 cup quinoa flakes

1 teaspoon dried oregano

½ teaspoon dried thyme

1 teaspoon dried basil

canola oil, as needed

2 cups shredded mozzarella cheese (about 8 ounces)

2 cups grated Parmesan cheese (about 6 ounces)

2 tablespoons chopped fresh basil

kosher salt and black pepper

1. **For the Tomato Sauce:** Heat the olive oil in a large saucepan over medium-high heat. Cook the onion in the oil, stirring occasionally, until translucent, 5 to 7 minutes. Add the garlic and cook, stirring constantly, about 30 seconds. Add the oregano, thyme, and red pepper flakes, if using, stirring to combine. Add the red wine and cook until it is reduced by half, 3 to 4 minutes. Add the tomatoes and their juice, stirring to combine. Bring to a boil, reduce the heat to medium-low, cover, and simmer for 30 minutes. Turn off the heat and season to taste with salt and pepper. Leave on the burner, covered, to keep warm.

2. Meanwhile, in a small saucepan over high heat, bring the quinoa and water to a boil. Reduce the heat to low, cover, and cook until the water has been absorbed and the quinoa is tender, 10 to 12 minutes. Turn off the heat and let the quinoa sit for 5 minutes. Fluff with a fork, cover, and leave on the burner to keep warm.

3. Peel the eggplant; cut off and discard the ends. Slice the eggplant into ½-inch-thick rounds and lay them out on a wire rack set over the sink or a rimmed baking sheet. Sprinkle the eggplant slices with 2 tablespoons of the salt and let sit for 10 to 12 minutes. Flip the slices and repeat with the remaining salt. Rinse under running water to remove the salt, squeeze out the remaining liquid, and lay the slices out flat until ready to use.

4. Make the frying batter according to the recipe instructions, tripling the recipe. In a large zip-top plastic bag, shake together the quinoa flakes, oregano, thyme, basil, and salt and pepper.

5. Line a rimmed baking sheet with paper towels. Pour enough canola oil into a large nonstick skillet to cover the bottom by about ¼ inch. Heat the oil over medium heat until it shimmers. You can test the temperature by dropping in a tiny bit of frying batter; if it sizzles, the oil is hot enough. Working with 2 or 3 slices at a time, dip the eggplant in the frying batter, then add to the quinoa flake mixture, close the bag, and shake to coat the eggplant. Carefully place the eggplant slices in the heated oil. Cook until the underside is browned, 2 to 3 minutes, then flip and cook until the second side is browned, 1 to 2 minutes longer. Remove from the skillet and drain on the prepared baking sheet. Repeat with the rest of the eggplant slices, adding oil as needed. Keep the cooked slices warm in a 170°F oven.

6. Preheat the oven to 400°F. Coat a 9-inch square baking dish with cooking spray. Spread about ¾ cup of the tomato sauce evenly across the bottom of the dish. Add a layer of eggplant and sprinkle with ½ cup cooked quinoa, ¾ cup mozzarella, and ¾ cup Parmesan cheese. Repeat for a second layer, beginning with the tomato sauce. Add a final layer of eggplant and top with about ¾ cup tomato sauce, ½ cup mozzarella, and ½ cup Parmesan.

7. Bake for 10 minutes. Lightly coat a piece of aluminum foil with cooking spray, then remove the dish from the oven and cover it with the foil. Reduce the oven temperature to 350°F and bake until the eggplant is tender and the sauce is bubbling, 30 to 35 minutes longer. Remove from the oven and let sit for 5 to 10 minutes. Top with fresh basil to serve.

STUFFED PORTABELLA MUSHROOMS

Popular as an appetizer, stuffed mushrooms easily adapt to become a dinner entrée when you use large portabella mushrooms in place of buttons or creminis. In this version, quinoa adds great texture to the spinach-cheese filling. After eating this dish, you'll wish you had made a double recipe. SERVES 4

⅓ cup white quinoa, rinsed

⅔ cup vegetable stock or broth

4 large portabella mushrooms

3 tablespoons plus 2 teaspoons extra-virgin olive oil

½ small yellow onion, diced

2 medium cloves garlic, minced

1 (16-ounce) bag fresh baby spinach

½ teaspoon grated nutmeg

1 tablespoon balsamic vinegar

1 teaspoon soy sauce

¾ cup ricotta cheese

1 cup shredded mozzarella cheese (about 4 ounces)

½ cup grated Parmesan cheese (about 1½ ounces)

kosher salt and black pepper

TOMATO SAUCE

1 (15-ounce) can diced tomatoes

1 tablespoon extra-virgin olive oil

½ teaspoon red pepper flakes (optional)

kosher salt and black pepper

1. In a small saucepan over high heat, bring the quinoa and vegetable stock or broth to a boil. Reduce the heat to low, cover, and cook until the liquid has been absorbed and the quinoa is tender, 10 to 12 minutes. Turn off the heat and let the quinoa sit for 5 minutes. Fluff with a fork, cover again, and leave on the burner to keep warm.

2. **For the Tomato Sauce:** In a medium saucepan over medium-high heat, combine the diced tomatoes and their juice, the olive oil, red pepper flakes, if using, and salt and pepper to taste. Bring to a boil, reduce the heat to medium-low, and simmer until the juices are reduced and the sauce is fairly thick, 25 to 30 minutes. Turn off the heat, cover, and leave on the burner to keep warm.

3. Preheat the oven to 350°F. Line a rimmed baking sheet with parchment paper. Remove the mushroom stems, mince, and reserve. Using a spoon, gently remove the gills from the underside of each mushroom and discard. Lightly brush each mushroom top with ½ teaspoon of olive oil.

4. Heat the remaining 2 tablespoons olive oil in a large nonstick sauté pan or skillet over medium-high heat. Cook the onion, stirring occasionally, until translucent, about 5 minutes. Add the garlic and cook, stirring constantly, about 30 seconds. Add the minced mushroom stems and sauté until they release their liquid, 2 to 3 minutes. Stir in the spinach and nutmeg and begin

wilting the spinach. Add the vinegar and soy sauce and continue to cook, stirring occasionally, until the liquid has been absorbed, 3 to 4 minutes. Season to taste with salt and pepper. Transfer the mixture to a strainer and drain, pressing with the back of a wooden spoon to extract as much liquid as possible. Return to the pan, cover, and leave on the burner to keep warm.

5. In a medium bowl, stir together the ricotta and mozzarella cheeses. Fold in the cooked quinoa and spinach mixture. Adjust the seasoning with additional salt and pepper as needed.

6. Place the mushroom tops on the prepared baking sheet. Spoon approximately ½ cup of tomato sauce into each mushroom, top with about ¾ cup spinach-quinoa filling, and sprinkle on 2 tablespoons Parmesan cheese. Bake until the mushrooms are tender and the Parmesan cheese has browned, 25 to 30 minutes. Evenly divide any remaining tomato sauce among four shallow bowls and top with the mushrooms.

CHAPTER 9
Desserts

Quinoa…for dessert? Yep! We use quinoa in all its forms—flour, flakes, and the seeds themselves—to provide a new spin on traditional sweets. After all, how many times do you get to offer a "healthy" dessert?

WINTER

Maple Cake

Triple-Chocolate Bundt Cake

Cranberry-Cherry Tart

Not-So-Nutty "Peanut Butter" Bars

SPRING

Quinoa Carrot Cake with Maple
    Cream Cheese Frosting

Lemon-Glazed Pound Cake

SUMMER

Ginger-Peach Shortcake

Cherry-Almond Toaster Pastries with
    Almond Glaze

Funnel Cake Bites

FALL

Poached Pears with Spiced Quinoa

Pecan Thumbprint Cookies with
    Coffee-Caramel Filling

Apple Galette

Pear-Fig Crepes with
    Honey Mascarpone

MAPLE CAKE

At the end of a long day, relax in front of a fireplace with a slice of this cake and a mug of hot cider or a glass of Calvados, and you'll be enveloped by the warmth of winter's pleasures. **SERVES 8 TO 16**

2 cups quinoa flour

½ teaspoon salt

2 teaspoons baking powder

1 teaspoon ground cinnamon

¾ cup packed brown sugar

½ cup (1 stick) unsalted butter, at room temperature

2 large eggs, at room temperature

½ cup unsweetened applesauce

1 cup real maple syrup

2 teaspoons maple extract

MAPLE GLAZE

1½ cups confectioners' sugar, sifted

1 tablespoon real maple syrup

½ teaspoon maple extract

1. Preheat the oven to 350°F. Line the bottom of a 9-inch springform pan with parchment paper, and butter the paper.

2. In a medium bowl, stir together the quinoa flour, salt, baking powder, and cinnamon.

3. In another medium bowl, use an electric mixer to cream together the brown sugar and butter for 3 to 5 minutes, starting at low speed and gradually increasing speed as the butter beings to cream. Beat in the eggs, one at a time. Add the applesauce, 1 cup maple syrup, and 2 teaspoons maple extract; beat until combined, 30 seconds to 1 minute. Fold in the flour mixture, using a spatula, and combine thoroughly.

4. Pour the batter into the prepared pan. Rap the filled pan a few times against a counter to settle the batter and remove any air bubbles. Bake until the top is golden brown and a cake tester inserted into the cake comes out with only a few crumbs clinging to it, about 35 minutes. Remove from the oven and cool in the pan on a wire rack.

5. Cover the edges of a cake stand or serving plate with strips of parchment paper. When the cake has cooled, run a knife between the cake and the springform ring to loosen the cake. Remove the ring and the bottom of the pan. Transfer the cake to the cake stand.

6. **For the Glaze:** Place the confectioners' sugar in a small bowl. Stir in the maple syrup and maple extract to make a thick glaze. Pour the glaze over the cake, using an offset spatula to coat the cake and letting the glaze run down the sides. Let the glaze set and then remove the parchment paper. Slice and serve.

TRIPLE-CHOCOLATE BUNDT CAKE

Three types of chocolate—cocoa powder, baker's chocolate, and semisweet chips—go into this rich, not-too-sweet cake. We found that the distinctive flavor of quinoa flour actually nicely complements chocolate, a contrast that is deliciously illustrated here. **SERVES 8**

2 ounces unsweetened baker's chocolate

1½ cups quinoa flour

½ cup unsweetened cocoa powder

½ teaspoon baking powder

½ teaspoon baking soda

½ teaspoon salt

¾ cup (1½ sticks) unsalted butter, softened

⅔ cup sugar

3 large eggs

1 (6-ounce) container low-fat vanilla yogurt

CHOCOLATE GLAZE
1 cup heavy cream

about 1⅓ cups semisweet chocolate chips (8 ounces)

1 tablespoon cornstarch

1. Preheat the oven to 325°F. Spray an 8-cup Bundt pan well with cooking spray or rub generously with butter.

2. Melt the baker's chocolate in a double boiler over simmering water. Or, place the baker's chocolate in a small microwave-safe bowl and microwave for 30 seconds at 50 percent power. Stir and microwave for another 15 to 30 seconds at 50 percent power, until the chocolate is about half melted. Stir with a small spatula or a spoon until completely melted. Set aside to cool slightly.

3. In a medium bowl, sift together the quinoa flour, cocoa powder, baking powder, baking soda, and salt; stir to combine. Set aside.

4. In the bowl of a stand mixer fitted with the paddle attachment, beat the butter and sugar at medium speed until fluffy, 1 to 2 minutes. Scrape down the sides. Add the eggs one at a time, beating well between additions and scraping down the sides occasionally. Beat in the cooled melted chocolate, then the yogurt. Continue to beat until the mixture is fluffy, 2 to 3 minutes longer.

5. Gradually add the dry ingredients to the mixer bowl, beating and scraping down the sides after each addition. The batter should be very thick and fluffy.

6. Spoon the batter into the prepared Bundt pan and smooth it out. Rap the filled pan a few times against a counter to settle the batter and remove any air bubbles. Bake until a cake tester inserted into the cake comes out with only a few crumbs clinging to it, 40 to 45 minutes. Cool in the pan for 10 minutes on a wire rack, then invert onto a plate or the rack and cool completely before glazing.

7. When the cake is almost cool, make the glaze: In a small saucepan, heat the cream over medium-low heat until it just reaches a simmer. Remove from the heat, stir in the chocolate chips with a whisk, and continue whisking until the chocolate is melted and the mixture is smooth and satiny. (Return to low heat if the chocolate isn't melting.) Stir in the cornstarch and then pour the warm glaze over the cake. Let the glaze set before slicing and serving the cake.

CRANBERRY-CHERRY TART

My mother-in-law makes a cranberry pie every Christmas from a Time-Life cookbook printed in 1970. It's a dish I now look forward to each holiday season, thus inspiring me to make my own version using quinoa. The tart is wonderful served with vanilla bean ice cream.—KS　SERVES 8 TO 16

CRUST
1 recipe Quinoa–Rice Flour Pie Crust
(page 30)

¼ cup quinoa flour

1 cup chopped toasted pecans

FILLING
1 (12-ounce) bag fresh cranberries
(or frozen cranberries, thawed)

2 tablespoons quinoa flour

1 cup granulated sugar

¼ teaspoon salt

¼ cup chopped dried cherries

¼ cup dried cranberries

1 teaspoon grated orange zest

¼ cup cran-cherry juice

¼ cup unsalted butter, melted

TOPPING
½ cup quinoa flour

½ cup quinoa flakes

½ cup old-fashioned rolled oats

½ cup packed brown sugar

½ teaspoon grated nutmeg

⅓ cup unsalted butter, melted

1. **For the Crust:** Preheat the oven to 400°F. Spray a 9-inch pie pan with cooking spray, or grease it with butter.

2. Make the crust according to the recipe directions, adding the ¼ cup quinoa flour and 1 cup chopped pecans to the dry ingredients in Step 1. Bake as instructed and reserve.

3. **For the Filling:** Lower the oven temperature to 350°F. In the bowl of a food processor, combine the fresh or frozen cranberries, quinoa flour, sugar, and salt, pulsing about 10 times to begin chopping the cranberries. Add the dried cherries, dried cranberries, and orange zest, and pulse until the fresh or frozen cranberries are pea-size or smaller and the dried fruit is blended in. Add the cran-cherry juice and melted butter, pulsing 3 or 4 times to combine. Turn out the mixture into the pie shell and spread evenly with a spatula.

4. **For the Topping:** In a small bowl, stir together the quinoa flour, quinoa flakes, oats, brown sugar, and nutmeg. Add the melted butter and toss to coat the dry ingredients, then spread evenly over the top of the cranberry filling.

5. Bake until the filling is firm and the topping has browned, about 55 minutes. Remove from the oven and cool completely on a wire rack before serving.

NOT-SO-NUTTY "PEANUT BUTTER" BARS

These bars contain no peanuts, but strangely enough they take on the flavor of peanut butter—perfect for those who love the flavor of peanuts but cannot eat them for one reason or another. **MAKES 16 BARS**

2 cups quinoa flour

1 teaspoon baking soda

½ teaspoon salt

2 large eggs, at room temperature

1 cup packed brown sugar

½ cup granulated sugar

½ cup (1 stick) unsalted butter, melted

¼ cup unsweetened applesauce

1 tablespoon vanilla extract

CHOCOLATE GLAZE

1 cup heavy cream

1 cup semisweet chocolate chips (6 ounces)

1 teaspoon vanilla extract

1 tablespoon cornstarch

1. Preheat the oven to 350°F. Butter the bottom and sides of a 9 x 9-inch baking pan and lightly coat with quinoa flour.

2. In a medium bowl, whisk together the quinoa flour, baking soda, and salt.

3. In another medium bowl, beat the eggs, brown sugar, and granulated sugar with an electric mixer on low to medium speed until the eggs have thickened, 3 to 5 minutes. Add the melted butter and beat for 30 seconds. Add the applesauce and vanilla and beat to combine, 30 seconds to 1 minute. Fold in the flour mixture using a spatula and combine thoroughly.

4. Pour the batter into the prepared baking pan and bake until a cake tester inserted into the bars comes out with only a few crumbs clinging to it, 30 to 35 minutes. Remove from the oven and cool completely on a wire rack.

5. **For the Chocolate Glaze:** In a small saucepan, heat the cream over medium-low heat until it just reaches a simmer. Remove from the heat. Whisk in the chocolate chips until the chocolate is melted and the mixture is smooth and satiny, returning the pan to low heat if the chocolate isn't melting. Stir in the vanilla. Stir in the cornstarch and pour the warm glaze over the bars. Cool completely before slicing and serving.

QUINOA CARROT CAKE WITH MAPLE CREAM CHEESE FROSTING

Classic carrot cake takes on a nuttier flavor and a finer consistency when made with quinoa flour. With the quinoa, the applesauce, and the carrots, we think this is a healthier option than most traditional carrot cakes—although the rich cream cheese frosting certainly tips the scales back in the direction of sinful! SERVES 8 TO 10

2 cups quinoa flour

1 cup packed brown sugar

2 teaspoons baking powder

1 teaspoon ground cinnamon

¼ teaspoon salt

3 large eggs

1 cup unsweetened applesauce

¼ cup vegetable oil

2 teaspoons vanilla extract

3 cups peeled and grated carrots
(about 1½ pounds)

¾ cup raisins

MAPLE CREAM CHEESE
FROSTING

1 (8-ounce) package cream cheese

½ cup (1 stick) unsalted butter,
softened

3 to 4 cups confectioners' sugar,
sifted

2 teaspoons maple extract

1 cup chopped walnuts (optional)

1. Preheat the oven to 350°F. Grease two 8-inch round cake pans with butter or shortening, or cooking spray.

2. In a medium bowl, combine the quinoa flour, brown sugar, baking powder, cinnamon, and salt.

3. In the bowl of a stand mixer fitted with the paddle attachment, beat the eggs at low speed, increasing to medium. Beat in the applesauce, vegetable oil, and vanilla extract, scraping down the sides occasionally. With the mixer on low speed, beat in the carrots. Gradually add the dry ingredients, beating just until combined, scraping down the sides of the bowl as needed. Remove the mixer bowl and fold in the raisins using a spatula or a wooden spoon.

4. Divide the mixture evenly between the two prepared cake pans. Rap the filled pans a few times against a counter to settle the batter and remove any air bubbles. Bake until the cake springs back when touched and a cake tester inserted into the cake comes out with just a few crumbs clinging to it, 20 to 25 minutes. Cool in the pans on wire racks for about 10 minutes. Then turn the cakes out onto the wire racks to cool completely.

5. **For the Frosting:** Place the cream cheese and the butter in the bowl of a stand mixer fitted with the whisk attachment. Beat on medium speed until fluffy and well combined. With the mixer on low speed, gradually add the confectioners' sugar, mixing well after each addition,

A United Nations committee has proposed that 2013 be declared the "International Year of Quinoa," and a Bolivian representative has submitted a draft proposing an International Day of Quinoa in 2013 to promote quinoa's potential for helping to combat poverty worldwide.

until the frosting has a fluffy but spreadable consistency. Beat in the maple extract.

6. Place one cake layer on a serving plate and spread icing over the top. Place the second layer on top, then frost the top and sides of the cake. Sprinkle the walnuts over the top of the cake, if using.

LEMON-GLAZED POUND CAKE

We are both huge fans of lemony desserts, so making a quinoa lemon pound cake was a no-brainer. The propensity of quinoa flour to make baked goods dense works in this recipe's favor. This cake is delicious served warm—as we discovered when we couldn't wait long enough for it to cool—but the texture improves in a day or two. SERVES 8 TO 10 (MAKES 1 LOAF CAKE)

½ cup (1 stick) plus 5 tablespoons unsalted butter, softened

1 cup granulated sugar

1 teaspoon salt

4 large eggs

4 tablespoons fresh lemon juice, divided

1 teaspoon vanilla extract

1 teaspoon ground ginger

1¾ cups quinoa flour

1½ cups sifted confectioners' sugar

1. Preheat the oven to 325°F. Grease a 9 x 5-inch loaf pan with butter.

2. In a stand mixer fitted with the paddle attachment, beat the butter on medium speed until fluffy. Add the sugar and salt, then beat until fluffy and increased in volume, 2 to 3 minutes.

3. Add the eggs one at a time, beating after each addition and scraping down the sides of the bowl regularly, until the eggs are completely mixed in. Beat in 3 tablespoons of the lemon juice, the vanilla, and the ginger. With the mixer on low speed, gradually beat in the quinoa flour until just combined.

4. Pour the batter into the prepared loaf pan. Bake until a cake tester inserted into the cake comes out with only a few crumbs clinging to it, at least 1 hour. Let the cake cool in the pan on a wire rack for 15 minutes.

5. Remove the cake from the pan and place it on a serving plate. Place the confectioners' sugar in a small bowl and stir in the remaining 1 tablespoon lemon juice to make a thick glaze. Pour the glaze over the cake. Let the glaze set before slicing and serving. Serve warm or allow to cool completely. Store wrapped loosely in plastic wrap for up to 2 to 3 days.

GINGER-PEACH SHORTCAKE

There's nothing like biting into a peach—and having the juice run down your hand—to say "summer." This recipe highlights the bright flavors of fresh peaches. **SERVES 6**

1 recipe Quinoa Buttermilk Biscuits (page 21)

4 tablespoons granulated sugar, divided

4 large peaches

1 tablespoon minced candied ginger, plus more for garnish

3 tablespoons orange liqueur

mint sprigs, for garnish (optional)

WHIPPED CREAM
½ cup heavy cream

½ teaspoon vanilla extract

2 teaspoons confectioners' sugar

1. Preheat the oven to 350°F. Line a rimmed baking sheet with parchment paper.

2. Make the biscuits according to the recipe directions through Step 4, adding 2 tablespoons of the sugar to the dough. Scoop the dough onto the prepared baking sheet using a ½-cup measure, leaving 2½ to 3 inches space between biscuits. The dough should yield 6 biscuits. Bake until golden brown and cooked through, 20 to 25 minutes.

3. Peel and slice the peaches. Place the slices in a medium bowl, and squeeze in any juice you can get from the skins. Stir in the candied ginger, orange liqueur, and remaining 2 tablespoons sugar. Cover and refrigerate for at least 30 minutes before serving.

4. **For the Whipped Cream:** In a small chilled bowl, combine the cream, vanilla extract, and confectioners' sugar. Using an electric mixer on low to medium speed, beat until firm peaks form.

5. To serve, place a biscuit on a plate, top with about ⅓ cup of peaches, and spoon whipped cream over the top. Garnish with a colorful sprig of mint or some minced candied ginger, if you wish.

CHERRY-ALMOND TOASTER PASTRIES WITH ALMOND GLAZE

When we saw a food truck hawking homemade toaster pastries, we sensed a trend, and we thought the dense, nutty character of pastry dough made with quinoa flour would be an ideal foundation for toaster pastries of our own. This recipe features a cherry filling you make from scratch, but if you want to take a shortcut or make a variety of flavors at once, you can use dollops of jam. MAKES 8 TARTS

1 recipe Quinoa–Whole Wheat Pie Crust (page 31)

1 (12-ounce) bag frozen pitted cherries, thawed

2 tablespoons granulated sugar

1 tablespoon plus 1 teaspoon cornstarch

1 tablespoon water

1 teaspoon almond extract, divided

1 large egg

1 cup confectioners' sugar, sifted

1 tablespoon whole milk

¼ cup sliced almonds

1. Prepare the pie crust according to the recipe directions through Step 2.

2. Place the cherries in the container of a blender or food processor and blend or pulse until pureed but still slightly chunky. In a small saucepan over medium heat, bring the cherries and the sugar to a simmer. Reduce the heat to medium-low and simmer until syrupy, about 5 minutes. In a small bowl, combine the cornstarch and the water to make a thin paste, then add to the cherries in the saucepan. Simmer, stirring, until the mixture has thickened, about 5 minutes. Transfer to a heatproof bowl and let cool for 10 minutes, then stir in ½ teaspoon of the almond extract.

3. On a well-floured surface, roll out half the pie dough into a rectangle about ⅛ inch thick. Use a knife or pizza cutter to cut 3 x 4-inch rectangles, re-rolling the dough as needed; avoid working it too much, to keep it from getting tough. Roll out the remaining half of the dough and cut out more rectangles, trying to end up with an even total number of pieces. You should be able to get 16 rectangles from the dough.

4. To make the tarts, preheat the oven to 375°F. Line a rimmed baking sheet with parchment paper. Lightly beat the egg in a small bowl. Use a pastry brush to brush egg over one rectangle of dough, mound a heaping tablespoon of cherry filling in the middle of the dough, and lay another rectangle on top. Press down on the top piece, spreading the filling slightly and sealing the edges. Use the tines of a fork to crimp the edges, sealing them further and creating a decorative effect. Repeat with the rest of the dough and filling. Place the tarts on the prepared baking sheet and cut 2 or 3 slits in the top of each pastry to allow steam to escape. Bake until golden brown on the edges, 20 to 25 minutes. Remove from pan and let cool completely on a wire rack.

5. When the tarts are cool, make the glaze: Place the confectioners' sugar in a small bowl with the remaining ½ teaspoon almond extract. Gradually whisk in the milk a little at a time to make a thick glaze; you might not need all the milk. Spoon the glaze over the tarts, spreading it with a spatula. Sprinkle each tart with slivered almonds while the glaze is still wet. Let the glaze firm up completely before serving.

FUNNEL CAKE BITES

Adapted from the essential Quinoa Buttermilk Pancakes recipe (page 19), these bites bring the fun and flavor of a carnival home for any summer day.   SERVES 8 TO 12

¾ cup quinoa flour

¾ cup quinoa flakes

½ teaspoon kosher salt

1 teaspoon baking powder

1 ½ teaspoons baking soda

2 large eggs, at room temperature

¼ cup honey

¾ cup whole milk

¼ teaspoon cream of tartar

canola oil, as needed for frying

1 cup confectioners' sugar

1. In a medium bowl, whisk together the quinoa flour, quinoa flakes, salt, baking powder, and baking soda.

2. In two medium bowls, separate the egg whites from the egg yolks; set the whites aside. Whisk together the egg yolks, honey, and milk. Stir in the flour mixture until combined. Set aside for 5 minutes.

3. Beat the egg whites with an electric mixer on low speed until they begin to foam, about 1 minute. Add the cream of tartar, increase the speed to medium-high, and continue beating until medium peaks form, 1 to 2 minutes longer. Using a rubber spatula, gently fold the egg whites into the batter until just combined.

4. Fill a large heavy pot, such as a Dutch oven, with canola oil to a depth of 4 to 6 inches. Heat the oil to 300°F for frying. Line a rimmed baking sheet with paper towels.

5. Fill a pastry bag fitted with a medium tip with batter; or use a 1-gallon plastic freezer bag, cutting about ¼ inch off one bottom corner. Pipe batter into the hot oil until it loosely covers the surface. When the batter turns golden brown and you can see color coming up the sides from underneath, begin to break apart the pieces with tongs or a spoon. Continue cooking, turning as needed, until all sides are golden brown. Using a slotted spoon, remove the funnel cake bites to the prepared baking sheet. Repeat with the remaining batter.

6. Place the confectioners' sugar in a paper bag. Add the funnel cake bites, close the bag, and shake to coat completely. Remove and serve immediately.

POACHED PEARS WITH SPICED QUINOA

Look for pears that are ripe but firm to use in this fall recipe. If the pears are too ripe, they will begin to break down in the poaching process. Bartlett is our pear of choice. A fruity wine with a hint of spice, such as merlot or zinfandel, works well for this recipe. This dish can be served hot or cold. **SERVES 4 TO 8**

SPICED QUINOA

½ cup white quinoa, rinsed

1 cup water

½ teaspoon ground cinnamon

¼ teaspoon grated nutmeg

2 tablespoons dried currants

2 tablespoons diced dried apricots

2 tablespoons golden raisins

POACHED PEARS

1 (750ml) bottle red wine

1½ cups granulated sugar

2 cinnamon sticks

1 teaspoon whole cloves

1 teaspoon whole peppercorns

¼ cup orange juice or 1 orange, sliced

4 pears (such as Bartletts), peeled, halved, and cored

1. **For the Spiced Quinoa:** In a small saucepan over high heat, bring the quinoa and water to a boil. Reduce the heat to low, cover, and cook until the water has been absorbed and the quinoa is tender, 10 to 12 minutes. Turn off the heat and let the quinoa sit for 5 minutes. Fluff with a fork. Stir in the cinnamon and nutmeg. Add the currants, dried apricots, and golden raisins, and stir to combine. Cover and leave on the stove to keep warm.

2. **For the Poached Pears:** In a large saucepan over medium-high heat, place the wine, sugar, cinnamon sticks, cloves, peppercorns, and orange juice or orange slices, stirring to combine. Bring to a boil, reduce the heat to low, and simmer for 20 minutes. Carefully add the pears and cook until tender when pierced with a toothpick, 20 to 25 minutes. Remove the pears with a slotted spoon, drain, and reserve. Continue cooking the sauce until it is reduced to about 1½ cups.

3. For each serving, mound spiced quinoa in the center of a shallow bowl and lean 1 or 2 pear halves against it. Spoon the wine reduction around the quinoa and drizzle over the top.

PECAN THUMBPRINT COOKIES
WITH COFFEE-CARAMEL FILLING

We love the crust for the Cranberry-Cherry Tart (page 166) so much that we couldn't help but use it again to make these delicious cookies. You may certainly make smaller cookies than what the recipe calls for, but we love caramel and like a high caramel-to-cookie ratio. **MAKES 15 COOKIES**

COOKIES

1 recipe Quinoa–Rice Flour Pie Crust
(page 30)

¼ cup quinoa flour

1 cup chopped toasted pecans

COFFEE-CARAMEL FILLING

1 (14-ounce) can sweetened
condensed milk

½ cup (1 stick) unsalted butter, cut
into 1-tablespoon slices

1 tablespoon instant espresso

1. **For the Cookies:** Preheat the oven to 400°F. Line a large baking sheet with parchment paper.

2. Make the pie crust according to the recipe directions through Step 3, adding the ¼ cup quinoa flour and 1 cup chopped pecans to the dry ingredients in Step 1. Divide the chilled dough into 2-tablespoon portions. Roll each portion into a ball, flatten, and use your thumb and forefinger to press down the center to form sides about ¼ inch thick. Lay the cookies on the prepared baking sheet and bake until golden brown, about 12 minutes. Remove from the oven and cool completely on the pan on a wire rack.

3. **For the Coffee-Caramel Filling:** In a large heavy saucepan over medium heat, cook the sweetened condensed milk, butter, and espresso, stirring occasionally with a wooden spoon, until the butter melts. Continue to cook, stirring constantly, until the mixture has thickened to the point that when the wooden spoon is dragged across the bottom of the pan it takes several seconds for the surface to be covered with caramel again, 12 to 15 minutes. Remove from the stove and let cool completely.

4. Spoon cooled caramel into the center of each cookie so that it is level with the top of the sides. Let the caramel set completely before serving.

APPLE GALETTE

This rustic dessert makes a minimal but beautiful presentation that wows without anyone having to spend hours in the kitchen. It's a great option for entertaining; simply serve it warm with vanilla bean or dulce de leche ice cream. SERVES 8

1 recipe Quinoa–Whole Wheat Pie Crust (page 31)

1 cup apple butter

2 tablespoons spiced rum

1 tablespoon brown sugar

¼ cup (½ stick) unsalted butter, melted

2 large green apples (such as Granny Smith), peeled and cored

1 tablespoon granulated sugar

1. Preheat the oven to 400°F. Line a large baking sheet with parchment paper.

2. Make the pie crust according to the recipe directions. Roll out according to the recipe, but lay out flat on the prepared baking sheet.

3. In a medium bowl, whisk together the apple butter, spiced rum, brown sugar, and 2 tablespoons of the melted butter. Cut the apples into ⅛-inch slices. Add the apple slices to the apple butter mixture and toss to coat.

4. Layer the apple slices in concentric circles on the dough, starting in the center and going to about 2 inches from the edge of the crust. Fold the pie crust over the edge of the apples and pour any leftover sauce over the apples. Brush the remaining 2 tablespoons of melted butter over the pie crust edges and the apples. Sprinkle the sugar over the edge of the crust.

5. Bake until the apples are tender and the crust has browned, 30 to 35 minutes. Allow to cool on the pan on a wire rack for at least 10 minutes before serving.

PEAR-FIG CREPES WITH HONEY MASCARPONE

Apple cider can replace the dessert wine in this recipe, if you wish. Make sure the pears are ripe but still firm. You want the pears to begin breaking down while being sautéed but to remain mostly in cubes. **SERVES 6 TO 8**

⅓ cup dessert wine (such as late-harvest riesling)

1 cup chopped dried figs

1 recipe Quinoa Crepes (page 20)

3 teaspoons granulated sugar

2 teaspoons vanilla extract, divided

1 cup mascarpone cheese

3 tablespoons honey

2 large pears (such as Bartletts), peeled, cored, and diced

1 tablespoon fresh lemon juice

2 tablespoons unsalted butter

1 cup chopped toasted walnuts

¼ cup minced candied ginger

grated nutmeg

1. In a small bowl, pour the wine over the dried figs. Reserve.

2. Make the crepes, adding the sugar and 1 teaspoon of the vanilla to the batter. Following the instructions, cook the crepes. Reserve and keep warm in a 170°F oven.

3. In a small bowl, place the mascarpone, remaining 1 teaspoon vanilla, and honey. Beat with an electric mixer on low speed until combined, about 1 minute. Reserve.

4. In a medium bowl, stir together the chopped pears and lemon juice to combine. This helps prevent the pears from browning.

5. Heat a large nonstick sauté pan or skillet over medium heat. Melt the butter, add the pears, and sauté until tender, 1 to 2 minutes. Add the wine and figs and cook until the wine has almost cooked off completely, 3 to 4 minutes. Stir in the walnuts and candied ginger. Remove from the heat and keep warm in a 170°F oven.

6. For each serving, spoon ⅓ to ½ cup filling down the center of a crepe and roll up. Top with about 2 tablespoons of the honey mascarpone and sprinkle on nutmeg. Serve warm.

CHAPTER 10

Picnics, Packed Lunches, and Other Portable Goodies

Here you'll find versatile selections for snacks, lunches, and even leisurely weekend picnics. Instead of settling for another trip to the drive-through or the deli counter, try one or more of these recipes for a healthy change of taste.

Shrimp, Cucumber, and Quinoa Salad

Macaroni Salad

Pasta Toss with Sun-Dried Tomatoes, Olives, and Pine Nuts

Turkey-Cheese Hand Pies

Ham and Swiss Biscuit Sandwiches

Sun-Dried Tomato and Mozzarella Stromboli

Sausage-Cheddar Lunch Muffins

Falafel Sandwiches

Apple-Cherry Trail Bars

Congo Bars

Peanut Butter and Jelly Bars

SHRIMP, CUCUMBER, AND QUINOA SALAD

Cool, refreshing, and elegant—like something the hostess of a ladies' bridge club might serve—this salad is delicious presented in lettuce cups, hollowed-out tomatoes, or avocado halves. **SERVES 6 TO 8**

1 cup white quinoa, rinsed

2 cups water

1 (10-ounce) package frozen cooked salad shrimp, thawed

1 medium cucumber, peeled, seeded, and chopped into ½-inch pieces

1 medium red bell pepper, diced into ¼-inch pieces

3 tablespoons fresh lemon juice

⅛ teaspoon kosher salt

1 tablespoon extra-virgin olive oil

2 tablespoons minced flat-leaf parsley

1. In a medium saucepan over high heat, bring the quinoa and water to a boil. Reduce the heat to low, cover, and cook until the water has been absorbed and the quinoa is tender, 10 to 12 minutes. Turn off the heat and let the quinoa sit for 5 minutes. Fluff with a fork and transfer to a large bowl. Cover and refrigerate until completely cool, stirring occasionally.

2. Add the shrimp, cucumber, and bell pepper to the chilled quinoa. Toss to combine.

3. In a small bowl, whisk together the lemon juice, salt, and olive oil. Drizzle the dressing over the quinoa mixture, add the parsley, and toss to combine. Serve chilled.

MACARONI SALAD

Macaroni salad is practically a prerequisite for picnics and barbecues. The piquillo peppers in this recipe can be found at most specialty grocery stores, but can be replaced with roasted red peppers or pimento peppers if desired. **SERVES 8 OR MORE**

1 (8-ounce) box quinoa macaroni

1 tablespoon extra-virgin olive oil

2 ribs celery, diced

1 medium carrot, peeled and shredded

1 cup frozen peas, thawed

¼ cup sliced green onion

¼ cup chopped flat-leaf parsley

1 cup shredded sharp cheddar cheese (about 4 ounces)

½ cup diced roasted piquillo peppers

DRESSING

½ cup mayonnaise

¼ cup sour cream

2 teaspoons dry mustard

1 tablespoon white wine vinegar

1 teaspoon honey

kosher salt and black pepper

1. Cook the pasta according to the package instructions. Drain, then rinse with cold water. Transfer to a bowl, toss with the olive oil, cover with plastic wrap, and refrigerate, stirring occasionally, until completely cool.

2. Add the celery, carrot, peas, green onion, parsley, cheese, and peppers to the pasta, stirring to combine.

3. **For the Dressing:** In a small bowl, whisk together the mayonnaise, sour cream, and dry mustard. Whisk in the white wine vinegar and honey. Season to taste with salt and pepper. Using a spatula, fold the dressing into the pasta salad to coat. Adjust the seasoning with additional salt and pepper, as needed. Serve cold.

PASTA TOSS WITH SUN-DRIED TOMATOES, OLIVES, AND PINE NUTS

Delicious warm, at room temperature, or chilled, this pasta salad is very easy to put together with a few ingredients that you can keep on hand in your pantry. It's terrific to pack for lunch or a picnic, or to eat at home as a light supper. SERVES 4 TO 6

1 (8-ounce) box quinoa pasta, such as macaroni, rotelle, or shells

½ cup chopped sun-dried tomatoes

⅓ cup toasted pine nuts

½ cup chopped ripe olives (preferably oil-cured)

¼ cup extra-virgin olive oil

½ cup grated Parmesan cheese (about 1½ ounces)

1. Fill a large pot with water and bring to a boil over high heat. Add the pasta and sun-dried tomatoes and cook according to the pasta package directions until the pasta is al dente, 8 to 10 minutes.

2. Drain the pasta and tomatoes in a colander, then return them to the pot or transfer to a serving bowl. Add the pine nuts and olives, tossing to combine. Drizzle with the olive oil and stir to combine. Sprinkle with about two-thirds of the Parmesan cheese and toss to distribute the cheese. Sprinkle the remaining cheese over the pasta. Serve warm, or cover and refrigerate until ready to serve.

TURKEY-CHEESE HAND PIES

*These handheld meals are wonderful for lunch, picnics, or any other occasion when
you might need to eat on the go. Use leftover turkey or chicken, or poach some just for the
occasion. Meat from a rotisserie chicken also works great.* MAKES 6 HAND PIES

¾ pound cooked turkey, diced

1 ½ cups frozen mixed vegetables,
thawed

½ cup low-fat cream cheese, at room
temperature

½ teaspoon kosher salt

1 teaspoon dried thyme

¾ cup shredded cheddar cheese
(about 3 ounces)

2 recipes (2 crusts) Quinoa–Whole
Wheat Pie Crust dough (page 31)

1. Preheat the oven to 375°F. Line a rimmed baking
sheet with parchment paper. In a bowl, combine the
turkey, vegetables, cream cheese, salt, thyme, and
cheese. Set aside.

2. Prepare the pie crust according to the recipe
instructions through Step 2, making a double batch. On
a well-floured work surface, roll out the cold pie dough
to about ⅛ inch thick. Cut rounds of about 6 inches in
diameter (use a personal-size pie cutter or a bowl or
plate as a guide, or cut out a paper template).

3. Place about ¼ cup filling on half of each round,
leaving a border to seal the edge. Moisten the edge of
the dough with water and fold the other half over the
filling. Use your fingers or the tines of a fork to crimp
the edges and seal them shut. Using a sharp paring
knife, cut a few slits in the top of each pie to allow
steam to escape. Transfer the hand pies to the prepared
baking sheet.

4. Bake until golden, 20 to 25 minutes. Serve warm or
at room temperature.

HAM AND SWISS
BISCUIT SANDWICHES

The essential Quinoa Buttermilk Biscuits (page 21) are a delicious vehicle for jazzed-up ham and cheese sandwiches. As a variation, stir a tablespoon or two of fresh chopped herbs, such as parsley or chives, into the dough before forming the biscuits. **Serves 6**

1 recipe Quinoa Buttermilk Biscuits (page 21)

2 tablespoons grainy mustard

2 tablespoons mayonnaise

6 thick slices roasted ham (about 2 ounces each)

6 slices Swiss cheese

1 large tomato, thinly sliced

6 romaine lettuce leaves

1. Preheat the oven to 350°F. Spray a rimmed baking sheet with cooking spray. Make the biscuits according to the recipe instructions through Step 4. Scoop the dough onto the baking sheet with a ½-cup measure, leaving 2½ to 3 inches between biscuits. The dough should yield 6 biscuits. Bake until golden brown and cooked through, 20 to 25 minutes. Allow to cool.

2. In a small bowl, stir together the mustard and mayonnaise. Carefully slice each biscuit in half horizontally.

3. Spread the mustard mixture over the cut sides of each biscuit. Build a sandwich by layering a slice of ham, a slice of cheese, a tomato slice, and a piece of lettuce on the bottom half of each biscuit, then topping with the other half. Keep the sandwiches cold until ready to eat.

SUN-DRIED TOMATO AND MOZZARELLA STROMBOLI

This festive pinwheel bread is a great snack or handheld lunch. Transport it whole, along with a serrated knife, and slice it at your destination so it stays fresh. You can experiment with fillings, using different cheeses and other ingredients—try chopped prosciutto, nuts, capers, anchovies, or basil. **SERVES 6 TO 8**

1 recipe Quinoa Pizza Dough (page 29)

1 cup shredded mozzarella cheese (about 4 ounces)

½ cup chopped sun-dried tomatoes

½ cup sliced black olives

1 teaspoon pizza seasoning

1 tablespoon extra-virgin olive oil

1 tablespoon sesame seeds

1. Prepare the pizza dough according to the recipe instructions. On a work surface lightly dusted with flour, pat the dough into a rectangular shape about 12 x 9 inches. Leaving a 1-inch strip uncovered at one long edge, sprinkle the dough with the cheese, tomatoes, olives, and pizza seasoning.

2. Line a rimmed baking sheet with parchment paper. Beginning with the long edge that's covered with toppings, roll the dough jelly-roll-style, as tightly as possible, ending with the uncovered edge. With the seam on the bottom, place the stromboli on the prepared baking sheet. Cover loosely with plastic wrap and let rest until it rises slightly, about 45 minutes.

3. While the stromboli is resting, preheat the oven to 375°F. Brush the top of the stromboli with the olive oil and sprinkle with the sesame seeds. Bake until crisp and golden, 30 to 35 minutes. Let cool on the baking sheet for at least 15 minutes before slicing. Serve warm or at room temperature.

SAUSAGE-CHEDDAR LUNCH MUFFINS

Savory muffins are the perfect handheld snack for a packed lunch, a grab-and-go snack, or a picnic. You can get creative with the add-ins to make this recipe your own; try different types of sausage or even chopped cooked ham, cooked ground beef, or turkey. Of course, the choice of cheese is up to you, too. MAKES 1 DOZEN MUFFINS

1 cup quinoa flour

1 cup cornmeal

1 tablespoon sugar

1 teaspoon kosher salt

2 teaspoons baking powder

2 large eggs

1 cup buttermilk

¼ cup (½ stick) unsalted butter, melted and slightly cooled

½ pound cooked sausage, such as Italian sausage or breakfast patties, casings removed

2 green onions, minced

½ cup diced red bell pepper (about 1 small pepper)

½ cup shredded sharp cheddar cheese (about 2 ounces)

1. Preheat the oven to 350°F. Spray 12 cups of a standard muffin pan with cooking spray, or line with paper liners.

2. In a medium bowl, use a fork to mix together the quinoa flour, cornmeal, sugar, salt, and baking powder. Whisk the eggs in another medium bowl, then stir in the buttermilk and melted butter. Pour the wet ingredients into the dry ingredients and stir until just combined. Stir in the sausage or breakfast patties, green onions, bell pepper, and cheese.

3. Spoon the batter evenly among the prepared muffin cups so they are about three-quarters full. Bake until the muffin tops are golden brown and spring back slightly when pressed, 30 to 33 minutes. Cool for about 10 minutes in the pan on a wire rack, then remove from the pan and place directly on the wire rack to cool completely.

FALAFEL SANDWICHES

These tender, moist falafel patties are a satisfying lunch packed with protein. The patties can be served warm, but they are a good picnic or packed-lunch option because they taste equally as good at room temperature or chilled. The falafel itself is gluten-free and vegan. SERVES 4 (MAKES 8 FALAFEL PATTIES)

⅓ cup white quinoa, rinsed

⅔ cup water

1 (15-ounce) can chickpeas, drained and rinsed

1 tablespoon fresh lemon juice

1 small yellow onion, diced

2 medium cloves garlic, minced

1 teaspoon ground cumin

½ teaspoon kosher salt

2 tablespoons chopped flat-leaf parsley

2 tablespoons chopped fresh cilantro

1 teaspoon chopped fresh mint

2 tablespoons extra-virgin olive oil

4 whole-wheat pitas

½ cup Hummus (page 51) or tzatziki sauce

4 butter lettuce leaves

12 cucumber slices

½ cup halved cherry tomatoes

1. In a small saucepan over high heat, bring the quinoa and water to a boil. Reduce the heat to low, cover, and cook until the water has been absorbed and the quinoa is tender, 10 to 12 minutes. Turn off the heat and let the quinoa sit for 5 minutes. Fluff with a fork and allow to cool.

2. Preheat the oven to 350°F. Line a rimmed baking sheet with parchment paper. In the bowl of a food processor, pulse the chickpeas until chopped, 12 to 15 pulses. Add the cooked quinoa, lemon juice, onion, and garlic, and pulse until just combined, 3 to 4 pulses. Add the cumin, salt, parsley, cilantro, and mint; pulse until the mixture is thoroughly combined, 6 to 8 pulses. Using a ¼-cup measure, scoop to form patties about 1 inch thick. Reserve.

3. Heat the olive oil in a large nonstick sauté pan or skillet over medium-high heat. Add the patties and cook until the underside is browned, about 3 minutes, then flip and cook until the second side is browned, about 3 minutes longer. Transfer to the prepared baking sheet and bake for 10 minutes.

4. To serve, cut the top off of each pita and spread about 2 tablespoons hummus or tzatziki inside. Place a lettuce leaf, 3 cucumber slices, and 2 falafel patties in each pita. Top with 2 tablespoons diced tomatoes.

APPLE-CHERRY TRAIL BARS

These chewy trail bars make great on-the-go snacks for kids and adults alike. **MAKES 24 BARS**

⅔ cup white quinoa, rinsed

1⅓ cups water

1 (12-ounce) carton frozen apple juice concentrate

1½ cups quinoa flakes

2 teaspoons ground cinnamon

½ cup roasted shelled unsalted sunflower seeds

1 cup chopped dried apple

1 cup chopped dates

½ cup chopped dried cherries

½ cup packed brown sugar

½ cup honey

¼ cup unsweetened applesauce

½ cup almond butter

1. In a medium saucepan over high heat, bring the quinoa and water to a boil. Reduce the heat to low, cover, and cook until the water has been absorbed and the quinoa is tender, 10 to 12 minutes. Turn off the heat and let the quinoa sit for 5 minutes. Fluff with a fork and allow to cool.

2. In a medium saucepan over medium-low heat, thaw the apple juice concentrate. Cook until reduced to about 1 cup, about 30 minutes. Do not let the juice concentrate simmer or boil, as it will burn. Remove from the heat and let cool.

3. Preheat the oven to 350°F. Line a 9 x 13-inch rimmed baking sheet with parchment paper or aluminum foil and coat with cooking spray.

4. In the bowl of a food processor, pulse the cooked quinoa, quinoa flakes, and cinnamon to combine, 2 or 3 pulses. Add the sunflower seeds, dried apple, dates, and dried cherries, pulsing 3 or 4 more times to combine.

5. In a medium bowl, whisk ¼ cup of the apple reduction with the brown sugar, honey, and applesauce. Stir in the almond butter. Add to the quinoa mixture in the bowl of the food processor and pulse to combine, 6 to 8 pulses. Turn out onto the prepared baking sheet and spread into an even layer, using a spatula. Bake until the dough is firm and beginning to form a crust on top, about 30 minutes. Remove from the oven and let cool enough to handle.

6. Reduce the oven temperature to 200°F. Turn out the dough onto a wire rack and remove the aluminum foil. Return the dough, on the rack, to the oven and cook until it begins to dry out, about 50 minutes. Remove from the oven and brush the top with the remaining apple reduction. Return to the oven and cook 10 minutes longer. Remove and cool completely before cutting into bars.

CONGO BARS

Our husbands grew up together in Atlanta, and their school often served Congo Bars for dessert. The treats were so popular that they still make appearances at alumni events. As a nod to their long-standing friendship, we developed our very own version of the dessert. MAKES 16 BARS

1½ cups shredded coconut

2 cups quinoa flour

1 teaspoon baking soda

½ teaspoon salt

¾ cup chopped toasted pecans

1 cup packed brown sugar

½ cup granulated sugar

½ cup (1 stick) unsalted butter, melted

2 large eggs

1 tablespoon vanilla extract

¼ cup unsweetened applesauce

½ cup semisweet chocolate chips (3 ounces)

½ cup butterscotch chips (3 ounces)

1. Preheat the oven to 350°F. Spread the coconut on a rimmed nonstick baking sheet. Toast in the oven until golden brown, 5 to 6 minutes, stirring halfway through. Remove from the oven and let cool.

2. Line the bottom of a 9 x 9-inch baking dish with parchment paper or aluminum foil and coat with cooking spray. In a medium bowl, stir together the quinoa flour, baking soda, salt, pecans, and toasted coconut.

3. In a small bowl, stir together the brown sugar, granulated sugar, and melted butter.

4. In a large bowl, whisk the eggs until well blended. Whisk in the vanilla and applesauce. Add the sugar mixture to the egg mixture, whisking to combine. Stir in the quinoa flour mixture. Fold the chocolate chips and butterscotch chips into the batter using a spatula.

5. Transfer the batter to the prepared baking dish, smooth with a spatula, and bake until the top is golden brown and a cake tester inserted into the bars comes out with only a few crumbs clinging to it, 30 to 35 minutes. Let cool completely in the pan before cutting.

PEANUT BUTTER AND JELLY BARS

Cut these gooey bar cookies into small pieces; they're very rich, so a little goes a long way. We used blackberry jam, but raspberry, strawberry, or grape would be just as yummy. Be sure to let the bars cool completely in the pan before attempting to cut them, or they'll fall apart. In fact, making these bars the day before you plan to serve them would be ideal. MAKES 24 BARS

2½ cups quinoa flakes, divided

1 cup quinoa flour

¾ cup plus ⅓ cup packed brown sugar, divided

1 teaspoon baking powder

1½ teaspoons ground cinnamon, divided

1 cup (2 sticks) unsalted butter, divided

⅓ cup slivered almonds

1 cup creamy peanut butter

1 (18-ounce) jar blackberry jam (about 2¼ cups)

1. Preheat the oven to 350°F. Butter a 9 x 13-inch baking pan or coat with cooking spray. In a medium bowl, whisk together 1½ cups of the quinoa flakes, the quinoa flour, ¾ cup of the brown sugar, the baking powder, and the cinnamon. Using a pastry cutter, two knives, or your fingers, work ¾ cup (1½ sticks) of the butter into the dry ingredients until the mixture resembles coarse crumbs. Press in an even layer into the prepared pan. Bake until set, about 10 minutes.

2. Meanwhile, make the topping for the bars by combining the remaining 1 cup quinoa flakes, the remaining ⅓ cup brown sugar, and the almonds. Melt the remaining 4 tablespoons butter in the microwave or in a small pan on the stovetop and pour it into the quinoa flake mixture. Stir to combine completely.

3. Remove the crust from the oven and spread the peanut butter evenly over it, then spread the jam over the peanut butter. If the jam doesn't spread easily, stir it in a bowl until it has a more spreadable consistency. Sprinkle the topping over the jam and return the pan to the oven. Bake until the topping is golden, about 20 minutes longer. Let cool completely in the pan before cutting.

CHAPTER 11

Parties, Potlucks, and Presents

What to make? What to make? That's the toughest question to answer when you're the host of a party, want to bring a potluck dish that will impress, or need to come up with a gift idea. The recipes in this chapter will help you create a tasty dish that won't be duplicated—and is sure to generate some good conversation. We even include quinoa "mixes" that you can package to offer as a hostess gift or give to a favorite teacher.

PARTIES AND POTLUCKS

Proscuitto-Fontina Breakfast Casserole

Croque Monsieur Crepe Stack

Puttanesca Bake

Kale-Gouda Bake

Mexican Seven-Layer Casserole

Mini Pizzas

Spicy Quinoa and Black Bean Salad

Quinoa-Corn Pudding

PRESENTS

Quinoa Pancake Mix

Herbed Quinoa Pilaf Mix

Ginger Biscotti

Cranberry-Orange Tea Bread

Rich Chocolate-Zucchini Bread

Walnut Wedding Cookies

PROSCIUTTO-FONTINA BREAKFAST CASSEROLE

This dish is more like a quiche than a typical casserole. Cooked asparagus, black olives, cooked bacon, or roasted red peppers would all be excellent substitutions or additions, and any firm or semi-firm cheese that melts well—such as Colby, Swiss, or Gouda—would work nicely. SERVES 8 TO 10

1 cup red quinoa, rinsed

2 cups water

8 large eggs, divided

½ cup pine nuts, ground in a food processor or spice grinder

1 teaspoon kosher salt, divided

black pepper

4 ounces prosciutto, chopped

1 tablespoon chopped chives

1½ cups shredded fontina cheese, divided (4 ounces)

2 cups whole milk

1 cup heavy cream

⅛ teaspoon grated nutmeg

1. Preheat the oven to 375°F. Grease an 11 x 7-inch casserole or baking dish or cover with cooking spray. In a medium saucepan over high heat, bring the quinoa and water to a boil. Reduce the heat to low, cover, and cook until the water has been absorbed and the quinoa is tender, 18 to 20 minutes. Turn off the heat and let the quinoa sit for 5 minutes. Fluff with a fork and transfer to a medium bowl to let cool for 10 to 15 minutes, stirring occasionally to hasten the cooling.

2. In a small bowl, lightly beat 2 of the eggs. Add the beaten eggs to the cooked quinoa along with the pine nuts, ½ teaspoon of the salt, and a few grinds or a pinch of black pepper. Press the mixture evenly into the prepared baking dish, smoothing the top with a spatula. Bake until the crust is firm, about 20 minutes. Remove from the oven and reduce the oven temperature to 325°F.

3. Sprinkle the prosciutto, chives, and 1 cup of the cheese evenly over the crust. With a whisk, beat the 6 remaining eggs in a medium bowl until smooth. Add the milk and cream, whisking to combine. Whisk in the nutmeg, the remaining ½ teaspoon salt, and a few grinds of black pepper. Pour the egg mixture over the crust and sprinkle with the remaining ½ cup of cheese.

4. Bake until the casserole is set and no longer jiggly, about 1 hour. Serve hot or warm. The casserole will keep in the refrigerator, covered, for 1 to 2 days. Individual pieces can be reheated in the microwave.

CROQUE MONSIEUR CREPE STACK

This fun dish is a clever interpretation of the French croque monsieur sandwich. With deli ham, Swiss cheese, and a Dijon cheese sauce, it has all the flavors of the original, but this version layers the filling between quinoa flour crepes to be broiled in the oven. Cut it into wedges to serve as an entrée or an appetizer. SERVES 12 TO 16

6 tablespoons unsalted butter

⅓ cup quinoa flour

2½ cups whole milk

1 tablespoon Dijon mustard

4 cups grated Jarlsberg cheese, divided (about 12 ounces)

2 recipes Quinoa Crepes (page 20), about 12 crepes

1 pound sliced deli ham

¼ cup chopped flat-leaf parsley

kosher salt and black pepper

1. Line a rimmed baking sheet with parchment paper. In a medium saucepan, melt the butter over medium heat. Sprinkle in the flour and whisk until it forms a paste. Gradually whisk in the milk until the mixture is smooth. Bring to a simmer, reduce the heat to low, and simmer, stirring occasionally, until the mixture has thickened, 10 to 15 minutes. Whisk in the mustard, then stir in 3 cups of the cheese, stirring occasionally until melted. Season to taste with salt and pepper. Turn off the heat. Cover and leave on the burner to keep warm until ready to use.

2. Prepare the crepes according to the recipe directions. For this recipe, they should be about 8 inches across.

3. Preheat the oven's broiler. To make the crepe stacks, place a crepe on the prepared baking sheet. Top with a piece of ham and a sprinkling of cheese. Drizzle a few tablespoons of the cheese sauce over the ham and cheese, then repeat with another layer of crepe, ham, cheese, sauce, and crepe. Drizzle the top with more cheese sauce and a sprinkling of cheese. You should end up with 4 crepe stacks (use a second baking sheet if they won't all fit on one).

4. Broil until the cheese is bubbly, 3 to 4 minutes. With a wide spatula, transfer to a serving plate, garnish with the parsley, and cut into wedges. Serve hot.

PUTTANESCA BAKE

A cross between pasta puttanesca and baked ziti, this is a flavorful option to pass out at a potluck. Just make sure that vegetarians know it contains anchovies—or you can omit them and simply add a tablespoon or so of capers. **SERVES 8**

1 tablespoon extra-virgin olive oil

1 small onion, diced

2 cloves garlic, minced

1 (28-ounce) can diced tomatoes

½ cup sliced black olives

6 tinned anchovy fillets, chopped

2 tablespoons tomato paste

½ teaspoon red pepper flakes, or to taste (optional)

1 (8-ounce) box quinoa penne

1 cup shredded mozzarella cheese (about 4 ounces)

kosher salt and black pepper

1. Preheat the oven to 350°F. Spray a 9 x 13-inch glass baking dish with cooking spray. In a medium saucepan, heat the olive oil over medium heat. Add the onion and sauté, stirring frequently, until translucent, about 5 minutes. Add the garlic and sauté for 30 seconds, stirring constantly. Stir in the tomatoes, olives, anchovies, tomato paste, and red pepper flakes, if using. Bring to a simmer, then reduce the heat to medium-low and simmer until the sauce is thickened slightly, about 20 minutes. Season to taste with salt and pepper.

2. Meanwhile, cook the quinoa penne according to the package directions. Drain and return to the pot. Pour the sauce over the penne and stir to combine. Spread the mixture evenly in the prepared casserole dish. Sprinkle with the cheese. Bake until the sauce is bubbling and the cheese is melted, 25 to 30 minutes. Serve hot or warm.

KALE-GOUDA BAKE

This deliciously cheesy casserole is inspired by a dish that our friend Elizabeth and her roommates used to make for dinner parties and potlucks—called, simply, The Bake. Full of healthy ingredients bought at their local food co-op, it was always a hit, especially on chilly fall days. If you like smoked Gouda, you can use it for about a quarter or a third of the cheese to add a nice smoky flavor, but it doesn't melt as well as regular Gouda. **SERVES 8**

2 cups red quinoa, rinsed

4 cups water

1 tablespoon extra-virgin olive oil

1 medium yellow onion, diced

1 bunch kale, chopped

4 large eggs

1½ cups cottage cheese

2 cups shredded Gouda cheese, divided (8 ounces)

⅛ teaspoon grated nutmeg

½ teaspoon salt

⅛ teaspoon ground black pepper

1½ cups frozen peas, thawed

1. Preheat the oven to 400°F. Spray a 9 x 13-inch glass baking dish with cooking spray.

2. In a medium saucepan over high heat, bring the quinoa and water to a boil. Reduce the heat to low, cover, and cook until the water has been absorbed and the quinoa is tender, 18 to 20 minutes. Turn off the heat and let the quinoa sit for 5 minutes. Fluff with a fork and allow to cool.

3. In a large nonstick skillet, heat the olive oil over medium heat. Add the onion and sauté, stirring frequently, until translucent, about 5 minutes. Add the kale and cook, turning with tongs, until wilted, 4 to 5 minutes. Remove from the heat and let cool slightly.

4. In a large mixing bowl, beat the eggs. Stir in the cottage cheese, 1¼ cups of the Gouda cheese, nutmeg, salt, and pepper. Stir in the cooked quinoa, kale, and peas. Spoon the mixture into the prepared baking dish, pressing down lightly with the back of a spoon or spatula to lightly compress and to even it out. Sprinkle the remaining ¾ cup Gouda cheese evenly over the casserole. Bake until the casserole is cooked through and the cheese is melted, 40 to 50 minutes. Serve hot.

MEXICAN SEVEN-LAYER CASSEROLE

This festive casserole is a riff on the popular party dip. With its cornmeal-quinoa crust, you can eat it on its own as a casserole, or you can serve it with tortilla chips. The "seven-layer" moniker is just a loose suggestion—feel free to add and subtract toppings as you wish. Yummy additions could include fresh cilantro, sliced green onions, diced jalapeño peppers, and diced red onion. **SERVES 8 TO 10**

1 cup white quinoa, rinsed

2 cups water

¾ cup cornmeal

1 teaspoon ground cumin

¼ teaspoon salt

¾ teaspoon chili powder

3 large eggs

2 (16-ounce) cans refried beans

¼ cup jarred salsa

1 cup prepared guacamole

½ cup sour cream or plain yogurt

1 tablespoon lime juice (from about ½ lime)

1½ cups shredded Colby cheese (about 5 ounces)

2 cups shredded iceberg lettuce

2 medium globe (slicing) tomatoes, chopped

1 (4.5-ounce) can sliced black olives, drained

1. In a medium saucepan over high heat, bring the quinoa and water to a boil. Reduce the heat to low, cover, and cook until the water has been absorbed and the quinoa is tender, 10 to 12 minutes. Turn off the heat and let the quinoa sit for 5 minutes. Fluff with a fork. Transfer to a large mixing bowl and let cool to room temperature, stirring occasionally to keep the quinoa from clumping.

2. Preheat the oven to 375°F. Spray a 9 x 13-inch glass casserole dish with cooking spray.

3. Add the cornmeal, cumin, salt, and chili powder to the cooked quinoa and stir to combine. Beat the eggs in a small bowl, then pour into the quinoa mixture and stir to combine. Spread the mixture in the prepared baking dish, pressing down lightly with the back of a spatula to even it out. Bake until firm, about 20 minutes.

4. While the crust is baking, heat the beans in a medium saucepan over medium-low heat. Stir in the salsa. In a small bowl, mix together the guacamole, sour cream or yogurt, and lime juice.

5. When the crust has baked, remove it from the oven and spread the beans over the top. Sprinkle the cheese on top and return the dish to the oven. Cook until the cheese is melted, 5 to 10 minutes.

6. Remove from the oven and spread the guacamole mixture over the casserole. Top with the lettuce, tomatoes, and black olives. Serve hot or warm.

MINI PIZZAS

Pizza is always fun, but mini pizzas are even more fun! You can make these any size you want, from bite-size versions perfect as hors d'oeuvres to larger pies, perhaps 6 inches, meant to be single-serving meals. For even more fun, bake the crusts ahead of time and let guests top their own pizzas with their favorite toppings. This makes a good vegetarian option, since everyone chooses what to put on their own pizzas. SERVES 6 TO 12, DEPENDING ON PIZZA SIZE

2 recipes Quinoa Pizza Dough (page 29)

cornmeal or semolina flour, for baking sheet

¼ cup extra-virgin olive oil

garlic powder or garlic bread seasoning

1 (24- to 26-ounce) jar prepared pizza or pasta sauce

2 cups shredded mozzarella cheese (about 6 ounces)

PIZZA TOPPINGS
sliced black olives, sliced pepperoni, diced green peppers, sliced banana peppers, sliced mushrooms

1. Prepare the pizza dough according to the recipe instructions.

2. Preheat the oven to 450°F. Dust a baking sheet with cornmeal or semolina flour. Divide the dough into equal-size pieces, anywhere from golf ball to baseball size, depending on how many people you're serving and how large you want the pizzas to be. Press or roll each piece into a circle about ¼ inch thick.

3. Arrange the dough circles on the prepared baking sheet (use a second baking sheet if they don't all fit) and lightly brush each crust with olive oil, then sprinkle with garlic powder. Bake until the crusts are golden, 10 to 15 minutes.

4. Remove from the oven and spread tomato sauce over each crust. Sprinkle with mozzarella cheese and top with the toppings of your choice. Return the pizzas to the oven and bake until the cheese is melted, 7 to 10 minutes longer. Serve hot.

SPICY QUINOA AND BLACK BEAN SALAD

This recipe was shared with us by Nidhi Mehta-Joshi, a co-worker of my stepmother, Pam. Nidhi is a vegetarian and loves cooking with quinoa. This spicy salad is a favorite to bring to office parties and other potlucks.—JH **SERVES 8**

2 cups white quinoa, rinsed

4 cups vegetable stock or broth

½ teaspoon cayenne pepper

2 teaspoons extra-virgin olive oil

2 small yellow onions, chopped

2 medium tomatoes, such as beefsteak, chopped

2 teaspoons ground cumin

3 cloves garlic, minced

2 cups canned or frozen corn, drained or thawed

2 cans black beans, drained and rinsed

2 medium bell peppers, chopped (preferably red and/or orange, for color)

¾ cup chopped fresh cilantro

1 tablespoon plus 2 teaspoons fresh lemon juice

kosher salt and black pepper

1. In a medium saucepan, combine the quinoa, vegetable stock or broth, cayenne pepper, and a pinch each of salt and black pepper. Bring to a boil over high heat, then reduce the heat to low, cover, and cook until the liquid has been absorbed and the quinoa is tender, 10 to 12 minutes. Turn off the heat and let the quinoa sit for 5 minutes. Fluff with a fork and allow to cool.

2. Meanwhile, heat the olive oil in a large nonstick skillet over medium heat. Add the onions, tomatoes, cumin, and garlic, and sauté until lightly browned, 7 to 9 minutes.

3. Transfer the cooked quinoa to a large serving bowl. Stir in the corn, black beans, bell peppers, cilantro, and lemon juice. Add the tomato mixture and stir well to combine. Season to taste with salt and pepper. Serve at room temperature or chilled.

QUINOA-CORN PUDDING

This side dish serves a crowd and is a nice accompaniment to a broad variety of dishes. Thawed frozen corn kernels may be used in this recipe instead of the fresh corn. SERVES 8 TO 12

½ cup (1 stick) unsalted butter

1 medium yellow onion, diced

½ cup green onion, thinly sliced, green parts only

kernels from 5 ears fresh corn (about 5 cups)

pinch of white pepper

1 cup quinoa flakes

½ teaspoon kosher salt

2 cups whole milk, divided

4 large eggs

2 tablespoons granulated sugar

1 cup heavy cream

1 cup shredded sharp cheddar cheese (about 4 ounces)

1. In a large nonstick sauté pan or skillet over medium-high heat, melt the butter. Add the yellow and green onions and cook, stirring occasionally, until the yellow onion is translucent, about 5 minutes. Add the corn kernels and white pepper, stirring to combine. Cook until the corn is tender, about 5 minutes longer, remove from the heat, and reserve.

2. In a small bowl, combine the quinoa flakes, salt, and 1 cup of the milk. Set aside until the milk has been absorbed.

3. Preheat the oven to 350°F. Grease a 9 x 13-inch baking dish with butter. In a large bowl, whisk together the eggs and sugar to combine. Add the remaining 1 cup milk and the cream, whisking to combine. Stir in the quinoa flakes. Fold in the cheese, then the corn mixture.

4. Transfer the batter to the prepared baking dish. Bake until the top is brown and firm to the touch and a toothpick inserted in the pudding comes out clean, 50 to 55 minutes. Allow to cool for a least 15 minutes before serving.

QUINOA PANCAKE MIX

This hearty pancake mix makes a great gift for a family to enjoy on a lazy weekend morning. What's more, it's also a good meal to take along on a camping trip. All you need to add is two fresh eggs—and for camping, you could even use powdered eggs. Dry buttermilk can be found in the baking aisle of most supermarkets. **MAKES 2 CUPS, ENOUGH FOR 6 TO 8 SMALL PANCAKES**

¾ cup quinoa flour

¾ cup quinoa flakes

½ teaspoon kosher salt

1 teaspoon baking powder

1½ teaspoons baking soda

3 tablespoons brown sugar

3 tablespoons dry buttermilk

Place all the ingredients in a large bowl. Use a whisk to combine them and break up any lumps. Store in an airtight container for up to 1 month.

Packaging Tips: This recipe makes about 2 cups of mix, which fits nicely into a 16-ounce canning jar. You could also pack it in a cellophane bag tied with a ribbon (look for food-safe plastic bags at a craft store or baking supply store), perhaps with a small whisk attached. Or arrange it in a gift basket along with a bottle of maple syrup or fruit compote. Include an instruction tag that says:

QUINOA PANCAKE MIX

To make a batch of pancakes, place the pancake mix in a large bowl. With a whisk, stir in ¾ cup water and 2 lightly beaten eggs. Heat an electric griddle or nonstick skillet and coat the surface lightly with butter or cooking spray. Spoon batter onto the griddle to form pancakes and cook for 4 to 5 minutes on each side, until the pancakes are browned and cooked through. Makes 6 to 8 small pancakes.

HERBED QUINOA PILAF MIX

We've been seeing quite a few packaged quinoa pilaf mixes coming onto the market—further proof that this superfood is here to stay. We love the convenience of not having to season and measure, so we created our own dry pilaf mix. You can use different types of herbs or bouillon to vary the results. **MAKES 1⅛ CUPS**

1 cup white quinoa

2 teaspoons dry chicken bouillon powder

2 teaspoons dried chopped onion

½ teaspoon dried thyme

¼ teaspoon garlic powder

Combine all the ingredients in a bowl. Transfer to an airtight container to store for up to 1 month.

Packaging Tips: Gift this mix in an 8-ounce jar, in a food-safe cellophane bag inside a cardboard window box, or in a Chinese take-out type of container. A wooden spoon would make a cute package decoration. Include an instruction tag that says:

HERBED QUINOA PILAF MIX
To prepare the pilaf, combine the pilaf mix in a medium saucepan with 2 cups of water. Bring to a simmer over medium-high heat, reduce the heat to low, cover, and simmer until tender, 10 to 12 minutes. Remove from the heat and let sit, covered, until the liquid has been absorbed completely, about 5 minutes. Fluff with a fork before serving. Serves 4 to 6.

GINGER BISCOTTI

These ginger biscotti pair beautifully with tea. For the coffee lover in your life, you can modify the recipe to make almond biscotti by eliminating the candied ginger, substituting almond extract for the vanilla extract, and adding ½ cup sliced almonds. MAKES 20 TO 24 BISCOTTI

2½ cups quinoa flour

½ teaspoon kosher salt

½ teaspoon baking soda

1 teaspoon baking powder

1 teaspoon ground ginger

3 large eggs

1 cup granulated sugar

1 teaspoon grated lemon zest

2 teaspoons vanilla extract

½ cup minced candied ginger

1. Preheat the oven to 350°F. Line a rimmed baking sheet with parchment paper. Sift together the quinoa flour, salt, baking soda, baking powder, and ginger into a medium bowl.

2. In another medium bowl, beat the eggs and sugar with an electric mixer on low to medium speed until the eggs have thickened, 3 to 5 minutes. Add the lemon zest and vanilla extract; beat on low speed until combined, about 30 seconds. Add the flour mixture and beat on low speed until just combined, 45 seconds to 1 minute longer. Stir in the candied ginger.

3. Turn out the dough onto a well-floured surface and form it into one long log, about 3 to 4 inches wide and 1½ to 2 inches thick. Place on the prepared baking sheet; if it doesn't fit, divide the log in half and use a second baking sheet.

4. Bake until the top of the log begins to crack and the center is cooked through, about 20 minutes. Remove from the oven and cool on the baking sheet on a wire rack for 20 minutes. Reduce the oven to 300°F.

5. Cut the roll into 1-inch slices and lay them out on the baking sheet. Bake for 20 minutes, then flip the slices over and continue baking until dry, 20 to 25 minutes longer. Remove from the oven and transfer to a wire rack to cool completely.

Packaging Tips: Stack the biscotti and wrap in food-safe cellophane, tied with raffia. Or look for vintage cookie tins at flea markets, line them with parchment paper, and pack with cookies.

CRANBERRY-ORANGE TEA BREAD

This sweet, citrusy bread is studded with fresh cranberries, which offer a juicy, tart surprise with nearly every bite. It's delicious toasted and spread with cream cheese. SERVES 8 TO 10 (MAKES 1 LOAF)

½ cup (1 stick) plus 5 tablespoons unsalted butter, softened

1 cup granulated sugar

1 teaspoon salt

3 large eggs plus 1 egg yolk

1 tablespoon grated orange zest

¼ cup orange juice

1 teaspoon vanilla extract

1¾ cups quinoa flour

1 cup fresh cranberries

1 cup chopped walnuts

1 tablespoon sanding (decorating) sugar or raw sugar

1. Preheat the oven to 325°F. Butter a 9 x 5-inch loaf pan. In a stand mixer fitted with the paddle attachment, beat the butter on medium speed until thoroughly combined. Add the sugar and salt, and beat until fluffy, 2 to 3 minutes.

2. Add the eggs one at a time, beating after each addition and scraping down the sides of the bowl occasionally, until the eggs are completely mixed in. Beat in the orange zest and juice and the vanilla extract until smooth and relatively lump-free, 3 to 4 minutes. With the mixer on low speed, gradually add the flour and mix until just combined. With a spoon, stir in the cranberries and walnuts.

3. Pour the batter into the prepared loaf pan and sprinkle with the decorating sugar or raw sugar. Bake until a cake tester inserted into the cake comes out with only a few crumbs clinging to it, 1 hour or longer. Let the cake cool in the pan on a wire rack for 15 minutes before carefully removing it from the pan. Cool completely on the wire rack before cutting.

Packaging Tips: Wrap this bread tightly in plastic wrap or clear, food-safe cellophane, then tie with a pretty ribbon. You can also bake it in a paper baker, which gives the bread a professional look. (Look for paper bakers in kitchenware or baking supply stores or online at sites such as www.kingarthurflour.com.) Cranberry-Orange Tea Bread makes a nice gift on its own or tucked into a basket with an assortment of teas and jams.

RICH CHOCOLATE ZUCCHINI BREAD

You'd never know that this dense, fudgy bread is (sort of) healthy! It was inspired by a favorite recipe from Cooking Light magazine that I make every year in the late summer when zucchini are bountiful. But luckily, you don't have to limit this bread to a summertime treat, since most supermarkets stock zucchini year-round.—JH SERVES 8 TO 10 (MAKES 1 LOAF)

⅔ cup packed brown sugar

2 tablespoons canola oil

3 large eggs

1 cup unsweetened applesauce

2 cups quinoa flour

3 tablespoons unsweetened cocoa powder

1½ teaspoons baking soda

1 teaspoon ground cinnamon

½ teaspoon salt

1½ cups shredded zucchini (about 1 medium zucchini)

1 cup semisweet chocolate chips (6 ounces)

1. Preheat the oven to 350°F. Grease a 9 x 5-inch loaf pan with butter, shortening, or cooking spray. Place the brown sugar, canola oil, and eggs in the bowl of a stand mixer fitted with the paddle attachment and beat at low speed until well combined. Add the applesauce and mix on low speed until combined.

2. In a medium bowl, whisk together the quinoa flour, cocoa powder, baking soda, cinnamon, and salt. Add to the mixer bowl and beat, beginning at the lowest speed and gradually increasing speed, until the ingredients are smooth and well combined. Using a spoon or a rubber spatula, fold in the zucchini and the chocolate chips.

3. Pour the mixture into the prepared loaf pan. Bake until a cake tester inserted into the bread comes out with only a few crumbs clinging to it, about 1 hour. Let cool completely in the baking pan on a wire rack before removing and slicing.

Packaging Tips: To give it a professional look, bake this bread in a disposable paper baker (look for them in kitchenware or baking supply stores or online, such as at www.kingarthurflour.com). Or wrap it tightly in food-safe cellophane or plastic wrap and tie with a ribbon. For a chocolate-lover's gift, package the bread with a few packets of hot chocolate mix.

WALNUT WEDDING COOKIES

This take on the classic Mexican wedding cookie is simple to make. These are just sweet enough to please most palates, making them great for a hostess gift, a holiday cookie exchange, or even a wedding favor. **MAKES 20 TO 24 COOKIES**

2 cups quinoa flour

1½ cups confectioners' sugar, sifted, divided

¼ cup granulated sugar

½ teaspoon salt

¾ cup (1½ sticks) unsalted butter, chilled and diced

1 cup chopped toasted walnuts

2½ teaspoons vanilla extract

3 tablespoons ice water

1. In the bowl of a food processor, add the quinoa flour, 1 cup of the confectioners' sugar, granulated sugar, and salt, and pulse 5 or 6 times to combine. Add the butter and walnuts and pulse about 15 times until the mixture resembles coarse crumbs and the butter is the size of small peas.

2. Add the vanilla extract and pulse 4 to 5 times to combine. Add the ice water 1 tablespoon at a time, pulsing until the dough clumps together. Turn the dough out onto a well-floured work surface and knead two or three times, just until it comes together. The dough should be slightly sticky; add more quinoa flour or ice water as needed to create the right consistency. Wrap in plastic wrap and refrigerate for 1 hour.

3. Preheat the oven to 350°F. Line a rimmed baking sheet with parchment paper. Divide the dough into heaping-tablespoon portions and form each portion into a ball. Place on the prepared baking sheet and bake until the cookies are golden and cooked through, about 25 minutes. Remove from the oven, place the pan on a wire rack, and cool until the cookies are cool enough to handle but still warm, 15 to 20 minutes.

4. Place the remaining ½ cup confectioners' sugar in a small bowl. Roll each cookie in the sugar to coat, adding more sugar to the bowl if needed. Place on a wire rack to cool completely.

Packaging Tips: These delicate wedding cookies should be packaged in a single layer in a bakery box (find various sizes at a craft or baking supply store) lined with parchment paper, or each cookie can be nestled in individual paper candy cups.

Appendix

Special Occasion Menus

New Year's Day Brunch
Banana Nut Power Muffins (page 36)
Black-Eyed-Pea Quinoa Pilaf (page 97)
Prosciutto-Fontina Breakfast Casserole (page 193)
Turkey-Cheese Hand Pies (page 183)
Quinoa, Bacon, and Blue Cheese Fritters with Horseradish-Yogurt Sauce (page 48)
Lemon-Glazed Pound Cake (page 170)

Valentine's Day for Two
Blini with Crème Fraîche and Gravlax (page 50)
Quinoa-Crab Salad in Lettuce Cups (page 54)
Goat Cheese Salad (page 70)
Honey-Glazed Duck with Fig and Pistachio Red Quinoa (page 140)
Triple-Chocolate Bundt Cake (page 164)

Summer Potluck Block Party
Sesame-Quinoa Cheese Straws (page 61)
Gouda and Red Pepper Tarts (page 52)
Shrimp, Cucumber, and Quinoa Salad (page 180)
Mexican Seven-Layer Casserole (page 197)
Peanut Butter and Jelly Bars (page 191)

4th of July Party
Macaroni Salad (page 181)
Quinoa Caprese Salad (page 73)
Grilled Quinoa Cakes (page 106)
Grilled Scallop Kebabs on Coconut Quinoa (page 132)
Cherry-Almond Toaster Pastries with Almond Glaze (page 172)

Thanksgiving Leftovers

Chicken Potpie with Quinoa Biscuit Crust (page 139)
Savory Turkey-Stuffed Crepes (page 142)
Turkey, Cranberry, and Quinoa Bake (page 138)
Turkey-Cheese Hand Pies (page 183)
Turkey "Waldorf" Salad (page 78)

Holiday Hors d'Oeuvres

Bacon-Wrapped Dates (page 64)
Eggplant "Caviar" on Grilled Quinoa Polenta (page 55)
Lamb Meatballs with Tangy Yogurt–Goat Cheese Dip (page 53)
Mini Pizzas (page 198)
Walnut Wedding Cookies (page 206)

Quinoa Manufacturers and Resources

These days it's easy to find quinoa at most supermarkets. If it's not in the aisle with the rice and grains, look in the natural foods section. It's also readily available at natural food stores either packaged or in bulk. White quinoa is the most common, but we've been able to find white, red, black, and tri-colored quinoa, as well as quinoa flour and quinoa flakes, in the bulk bins at our local specialty food stores, and we've seen bulk packages of white quinoa at warehouse clubs.

Alter Eco Americas, Inc.
San Francisco, California
(415) 701-1212
www.altereco-usa.com
This company aims to support developing producers around the world. They offer pearl (white), red, and tri-colored quinoa that is organic and fair-trade.

American Roland Food Corporation
New York, New York
(800) 221-4030
www.rolandfood.com
Roland sells prerinsed white, red, and black quinoa, along with flavored versions such as Black Bean Quinoa and Toasted Sesame Ginger Quinoa that are gluten-free. The company also sells kañiwa, a close relative of quinoa.

Ancient Harvest/Quinoa Corporation
Gardena, California
(310) 217-8125
www.quinoa.net
Under the name Ancient Harvest, this company sells organic white and red quinoa, quinoa flakes, quinoa flour, and gluten-free quinoa pasta.

Andean Dream
Los Angeles, California
(310) 281-6036
www.andeandream.com
This company offers organic, kosher, and gluten-free pasta made with a combination of quinoa and rice flour, as well as quinoa soup mixes and packaged cookies made with quinoa flour.

Arrowhead Mills
Boulder, Colorado
(800) 434-4246
www.arrowheadmills.com
Arrowhead Mills offers certified organic white quinoa.

Bob's Red Mill
Milwaukie, Oregon
(800) 349-2173
www.bobsredmill.com
Bob's Red Mill offers organic white quinoa and quinoa flour, as well as a seven-grain pancake mix that contains quinoa flour.

Earthy Delights

DeWitt, Michigan

(800) 367-4709

www.earthy.com

White and black quinoa are available from this specialty food site.

Eden Organic

Clinton, Michigan

(517) 456-6075

www.edenfoods.com

Eden quinoa is organically grown in the Andes Mountains on a family plot at a 12,000-foot plateau, and their production process uses techniques like mechanical de-saponizing (removing the bitter coating) and washing in mountain spring water. Products include white quinoa, red quinoa, bean and quinoa chili in BPA-free cans, and Twisted Pair, a kamut and quinoa pasta.

Indian Harvest

Bemidji, Minnesota

(800) 346-7032

www.indianharvest.com

This food service purveyor sells bulk black, red, and white quinoa to chefs and restaurants.

Pleasant Hill Grain

Hampton, Nebraska

(800) 321-1073

www.pleasanthillgrain.com

This natural foods website sells triple-cleaned organic white quinoa in bulk containers for home use.

SunOrganic Farms

San Marcos, California

(888) 269-9888

www.sunorganicfarm.com

This website supplies organic white, red, black, and tri-color quinoa along with an Italian quinoa blend.

TruRoots

Livermore, California

(925) 218-2205

www.truroots.com

The TruRoots quinoa is harvested in the salt flats of Uyuni, located in southwestern Bolivia. Organic white quinoa and organic sprouted quinoa are currently available.

Wholesome Kitchen

Flushing, New York

(718) 705-8203

www.wholesome-kitchen.com

This company makes quinoa mixes, including Dried Fruit and Nut, Vegetable and Smoked Paprika, and Lemon, Herbs, and Onion.

Zócalo Gourmet

Lynnwood, Washington

(425) 398-9761

www.zocalogourmet.com

This company, part of the Culinary Collective, which supports small-scale producers, offers quinoa, kañiwa (a relative of quinoa), quinoa flour, and kañiwa flour.

Conversions

MEASURE	EQUIVALENT	METRIC
1 teaspoon	--	5 milliliters
1 tablespoon	3 teaspoons	14.8 milliliters
1 cup	16 tablespoons	236.8 milliliters
1 pint	2 cups	473.6 milliliters
1 quart	4 cups	947.2 milliliters
1 liter	4 cups + 3½ tablespoons	1000 milliliters
1 ounce (dry)	2 tablespoons	28.35 grams
1 pound	16 ounces	453.49 grams
2.21 pounds	35.3 ounces	1 kilogram
325°F/350°F/375°F	--	165°C/177°C/190°C

Recipe Index

Acknowledgments

We'd like to thank the various quinoa experts and manufacturers who helped us while we were researching this book, particularly Roland Foods and Culinary Collective, who sent us samples and information; Cynthia Harriman from the Whole Grains Council, who let us pepper her with questions about quinoa; Vandana R. Sheth, RD, CDE, spokesperson for the Academy of Nutrition and Dietetics, who helped us with nutritional information about quinoa; and Sergio Nuñez de Arco of Andean Naturals, who helped us with historical information about quinoa.

And we are also grateful to the team at Ulysses Press for being so fantastic to work for, particularly our editor, Lauren Harrison, who is everything we could hope an editor would be: thorough, inspired, and most of all, patient.

—JH and KS

I am indebted to many people who helped me through the process of writing this book, beginning with Kelley, for being the perfect salt to my pepper in this project.

My parents, Judy and Greg Goldbogen, and parents-in-law, Joe and Christina Harlan, are, as always, unfailing supporters and advocates. My brother Jake and my siblings-in-law Steve, Rebecca, Ben, and Sarah, inspired me to include exciting meatless options within the book.

I'm always appreciative of my friends near and far, who contributed ideas and recipes, and who offered to test (or taste!) finished recipes. In particular, I'd like to recognize my dear friend Elizabeth Mangum-Sarach, who gave me the ideas for a few recipes and tested a few others. My college friend Caelyn Deeb-Diver shared with me how she's worked quinoa into Lebanese dishes, and my stepmom's friend Nidhi Mehta-Joshi also contributed her own interesting take on quinoa.

And finally, I am eternally grateful for my husband and daughters, who cheerfully and uncomplainingly ate meal after meal of quinoa. Their encouragement, compliments, and feedback buoyed my spirits.

—JH

First and foremost, I want to thank Jessica for asking me to collaborate on this cookbook. Not only did this experience allow me the opportunity to learn from her wealth of knowledge, but it gave me a reason to be in touch with one of my dearest friends nearly every day.

To my love, Adam Wisniewski, for his patience with, support of, and love for me. I am lucky to have such a wonderful husband by my side.

My love to and endless appreciation for my parents, Karen and Richard Sparwasser, who encourage me to dream but are always there to support me in reality.

To my in-laws, Sandra and Mirek Wisniewski, who welcomed me into their family with open arms and raised glasses.

I thank all of my friends for sending me encouragement, quinoa articles, and cooking experiences—even photos of quinoa shampoo! Very special thanks to Peg and Adolph Chiarpotti and Ashley Bisagne for their ideas, advice, and feedback on recipes; Rachel Rose for inspiring the lamb meatball recipe; Lisa Chuman and Lisa Rumbolz, from Seedy Bar, for tips on making trail bars; Grace Tanaka, from Baking with Grace, for her baking advice; and my mom's coworkers, for tasting many of my recipe test results and giving their opinions.

—KS

About the Authors

Jessica Harlan has written about food and cooking for nearly twenty years for many print and online publications, including About.com, *Clean Eating*, *Town & Country*, *Mobil Travel Guide*, Gaiam.com, *Pilates Style*, and *Arthritis Today*. A graduate of the Institute of Culinary Education in New York City, she has honed her skills and areas of expertise by developing recipes for major food brands, catering intimate parties, and getting involved in food-related charities. Her first cookbook, *Ramen to the Rescue*, was published by Ulysses Press in 2011. She lives in Atlanta, Georgia.

Kelley Sparwasser began a career devoted to food and wine in Portland, Oregon, where she completed cooking school and worked in area kitchens. She then moved to New York City and joined the editorial staffs of *McCall's* and the hospitality industry trade magazine *Food Arts*. After holding a public relations position at the Charlie Palmer Group, she opened a restaurant consultancy before returning to Oregon to pursue her passion for pinot noir as Direct Sales Manager at Penner-Ash Wine Cellars. Kelley holds the Advanced Certificate on Wine Studies issued by the Wine & Spirit Education Trust. She lives in Portland, Oregon.